"Ashley's doughnut recipes are some of the best I've ever tried, and I've tasted a heck of a lot of doughnuts. The peanut butter cup doughnuts are one of my go-tos—friends and family always go wild. You'll never know they are gluten-free!"
—JESSICA MERCHANT, FOUNDER OF THE BLOG HOW SWEET IT IS

"Every single doughnut craving—even ones you didn't know you had—will certainly be met in this beautifully photographed book. Best of all, Ashley's simple methods make creating mouthwatering baked doughnuts in your own gluten-free kitchen an easy task!"
—GRETCHEN BROWN, AUTHOR OF *FAST & SIMPLE GLUTEN-FREE*

"Everything about this gorgeous cookbook inspires us to dive into the world of homemade doughnuts. Best of all, these wonderful treats are baked and gluten-free, so there's truly something for everyone. Ashley's enticing recipes and beautiful photography had us drooling over every page."
—TODD PORTER AND DIANE CU, AUTHORS OF *BOUNTIFUL*

"With every type of doughnut and beautiful photos, Ashley has raised the bar in gluten-free baking for all of us."
—NICOLE HUNN, AUTHOR OF *GLUTEN-FREE ON A SHOESTRING*

"This is an excellent cookbook! No frying and no gluten, but still great texture and flavor. There's absolutely a doughnut for everyone and every occasion in this book!"
—LISA THIELE, FOUNDER OF THE BLOG WITH STYLE & GRACE

"*Baked Doughnuts for Everyone* is filled with fun, approachable recipes that will have you racing to the kitchen. From classic doughnuts, to savory, to decadent indulgences, Ashley has a way of making gluten-free baking fun for the whole family."
—JENNY FLAKE, AUTHOR OF *THE PICKY PALATE COOKBOOK*

BAKED DOUGHNUTS
for everyone

FROM SWEET TO SAVORY TO
EVERYTHING IN BETWEEN

101 DELICIOUS RECIPES
ALL GLUTEN-FREE

ASHLEY McLAUGHLIN

FAIR WINDS
PRESS
BEVERLY, MASSACHUSETTS

First published in the USA in 2013 by
Fair Winds Press, a member of
Quayside Publishing Group
100 Cummings Center
Suite 406-L
Beverly, MA 01915-6101
www.fairwindspress.com

17 16 15 14 13   1 2 3 4 5

ISBN: 978-1-59233-566-4

Digital edition published in 2013
eISBN: 978-1-61058-861-4

Library of Congress Cataloging-in-Publication Data

McLaughlin, Ashley.
  Baked doughnuts for everyone : from sweet to savory to everything in between, 101 delicious reci-pes, all gluten-free / Ashley McLaughlin.
      pages cm
  ISBN 978-1-59233-566-4 (pbk.)
 1. Gluten-free diet--Recipes. 2. Doughnuts. 3. Baking. 4. Baked products. I. Title.
  RM237.86.M39 2013
  641.81'5--dc23
                      2013024584

Book design by Rita Sowins / Sowins Design
Photography by Ashley McLaughlin
Author photograph by Laura Ramos, Fuse Photographic

Printed and bound in China

To my entire family.
Thank you for everything. Always. I love you all! xo

CONTENTS

baked doughnut basics

· ·

What is it about doughnuts? Their childhood comfort? The "doughnut Friday" rituals at work? Their cute round shape? The sprinkles? All of the above?

It's definitely all of the above. Doughnuts are that comforting treat we've always loved and always will. The only difference is that now you can enjoy them from the comfort of your own kitchen and without fussing over a fryer filled with hot oil. Not only are the recipes in this book a cinch to throw together, but they're also completely gluten-free—and totally delicious. So delicious, in fact, that no one will ever even guess the gluten is gone.

Gummy, grainy textures are a thing of the past when it comes to gluten-free baking. You won't find any of that here. This book uses a simple combination of flours resulting in a truly cake-like doughnut texture.

Are you prepared to bake your little heart out? Because once you start, you won't be able to stop. You will soon be known around town for your doughnut-making skills. Your family and friends will never love you more. Once you have a handle on the doughnut ingredients and process, let your imagination run wild with possibilities. They are endless!

My hope is for this book to give you comfort in the kitchen when it comes to gluten-free baking. It has never been easier or tastier. Time to roll up your sleeves, get a little messy, and most importantly, have fun!

DOUGHNUT TIPS AND TRICKS

While it was my goal to create simple, easy-to-follow recipes, it never hurts to explain a few tips and tricks to help you get things started right. These tips will help you create perfect baked doughnuts time and time again!

- I use Wilton brand doughnut pans (page 171) for my standard pan, mini pan, and twist pan. I use NordicWare brand for the doughnut hole pan. If you are using a different brand, the yield and bake time may vary.

- At the top of each recipe, you will find my recommendation for which type of pan to use. All baking times are based on a standard 6-doughnut pan and will vary when using other pans.

- Scoop flour into your dry measuring cups with a spoon and level off with the flat side of a butter knife for the best accuracy.

- It is important to not overmix the batter to avoid a tough texture. Stop stirring when you no longer see dry flour, and you'll be good to go!

- Substitute at your own risk! When baking, especially gluten-free, substituting any of the ingredients can lead to problems.

- The best way to grease your doughnut pan is with softened coconut oil, butter, or cooking spray.

- It is best to bake with ingredients that are all at room temperature. Taking ingredients out an hour before you start baking will do the trick.

- A thin, flexible spatula will help when removing the doughnuts from the pan. I like to use a silicone cookie spatula.

- Transfer the batter to the pan by carefully spooning it in or by scooping it into a gallon-size plastic bag, cutting a small tip off the end, and then piping it in the molds. Gently even out with a spatula.

- Whenever fruit is called for, use fresh, not frozen, unless otherwise specified.

- Whenever milk is called for, use 2 percent milk, unsweetened almond milk, or unsweetened soy milk, unless otherwise specified.

- Always let doughnuts cool completely before adding any toppings, unless otherwise specified.

- When measuring sticky ingredients such as honey, maple syrup, and molasses, coat the measuring cup with a light rub of oil or cooking spray and it will slide right out.

- For easier cleanup when topping the doughnuts, place foil, parchment, or waxed paper under the wire racks. This will help avoid a sticky, sugar-coated counter.

- Doughnuts are best made and served the day of baking, but if needed you can make one day ahead. Let the doughnuts cool completely and then wrap individually and store in a sealed container on the counter. Frost or decorate the day of serving.

- If you need your glaze to set quickly, place the glazed doughnuts in the fridge on a baking sheet for 15 to 30 minutes. Remove and let come to room temperature before serving.

- In case you a.) don't have a doughnut pan yet, b.) lost your doughnut pan, or c.) are anxiously awaiting one for your birthday that is 355 days away, not to worry. You can use a regular muffin pan or mini muffin pan instead. Just note that the bake time will vary. This will be our little secret!

- Coconut oil and coconut butter are two different ingredients. Coconut butter is a thick, buttery ingredient, made from the flesh of the coconut, whereas coconut oil is purely the oil extracted from the flesh. Both will liquefy around 76°F (24.4°C) and can change from liquid to solid and back again with no problem.

- You can make coconut butter at home with one simple ingredient: unsweetened finely shredded coconut. Place 3 cups (240 g) in a large-capacity food processor and process for 8 to 12 minutes or until you reach a drippy, smooth, and buttery texture. Scrape down the sides of the bowl as needed to keep the mixture moving. Let cool and then store in an airtight jar at room temperature. Note: Do not use sweetened or "lite" coconut and do not add oil, milk, or water.

- When using canned coconut milk, be sure to note whether the recipe calls for the lite or full-fat variety, as they are quite different.

- Coconut cream is the thick cream that sits on top of the liquid in full-fat coconut milk cans. It has an incredibly rich and smooth texture, almost as thick as whipped cream. To extract the coconut cream, place the can of full-fat coconut milk in the refrigerator for at least 2 hours or in the freezer for 30 minutes. Open the can (do not shake) and scrape out the coconut cream until you hit the liquid towards the bottom of the can. The liquid can be reserved and added to smoothies or savory dishes, such as coconut-based curries.

- Pure cane sugar is specified in the recipes, but feel free to use sucanat, coconut sugar, or white table sugar if desired.

- Did you know that powdered sugar is just finely ground cane sugar? It can easily be made at home with practically any type of crystalized sugar. To make, blend 1 cup (200 g) of pure cane sugar with 1 tablespoon (8 g) of arrowroot starch (or cornstarch) in your blender until you have a fine powdery texture, about 5 to 10 seconds. Store the sugar in an airtight container and use just as you would in any recipe calling for powdered sugar.

- I recommend tasteless, high-heat-safe oils, such as safflower oil, grape-seed oil, or sunflower oil, unless otherwise specified. Canola oil will also work. Source organic, cold-pressed, non-GMO oils whenever possible.

A GUIDE TO FLOURS

The flours used in this book can be found at most natural food stores or ordered in bulk online if you prefer. If you go with the latter option, just be sure to store any excess flour in an airtight container in the fridge to keep it fresh.

ALMOND MEAL

Almond meal is a gluten-free and grain-free flour ground from whole, raw almonds and is not to be confused with almond flour, which is made with blanched (skinless) almonds. It packs a hefty punch of protein, fiber, and healthy fats. Almond meal helps create a soft, moist texture in baked goods and is a crucial ingredient to the doughnut recipes in this book.

You can make almond meal at home by pulsing almonds in your food processor or high-power blender. It's best to grind in small batches (about ½ cup [73 g] at a time for 5 to 10 seconds) until you are left with a soft, finely ground texture. After grinding, you'll want to sift the flour and regrind any hard pieces that are left. Keep almond meal stored in an airtight container in the fridge. Note: Beware that if you grind too long the almond meal will start to heat up and turn into a paste, which will eventually give you almond butter.

COCONUT FLOUR

This is a naturally gluten-free flour derived from coconut meat. It is packed with healthy fats and fiber, so a little goes a long way. Coconut flour has no binding power and is a very dry flour. You'll find it used in most of the vegan recipes for texture enhancement. It does not substitute well for other flours and is not easily made at home.

GLUTEN-FREE OAT FLOUR

Oat flour is ground from the oat grain (also known as oat groats). Be sure to source certified gluten-free oat flour to ensure they have not been cross-contaminated with wheat in the growing or packaging process. Oats are a naturally gluten-free grain but are typically grown in close proximity with wheat fields. They are also commonly processed and packaged in the same facilities, opening up numerous chances for cross-contamination.

If you can't find certified gluten-free oat flour, or would rather make your own, you can do so by grinding gluten-free whole oat groats, gluten-free steel-cut oats, or even old-fashioned gluten-free rolled oats. Grind in small batches in a flour mill, high-speed blender (such as a Vitamix), or even a spice or coffee grinder, until soft and flour-like in texture. Sift and store in an airtight container in the fridge. If you are unable to tolerate gluten-free oat flour, you can substitute gluten-free all purpose flour at a ratio of 1:1.

GROUND FLAX MEAL

Ground flax meal is simply raw, ground flaxseeds. It acts as a binding agent to help hold the doughnuts together (especially in the vegan recipes) and adds moisture, healthy fats, and fiber as well.

You can buy it preground or grind from whole raw flaxseeds in your blender, coffee grinder, or flour mill. Grind in small quantities until you are left with a soft, fine texture (about 5 to 10 seconds). Avoid overgrinding as it will cause moisture and clumping. Sift after grinding and store in an airtight container in the fridge.

SWEET RICE FLOUR

This flour is very specific and offers no substitutions. It is quite different from white or brown rice flour, as it won't result in a grainy texture and is much starchier. It is ground from sticky white rice and helps give a doughy quality to the doughnuts. Another name for sweet rice flour is mochiko. Sweet rice flour is commonly found in the gluten-free aisle of your grocery store and in Asian grocery stores. It is also easily found online (page 171). My favorite brand is by Ener-G.

CHAPTER 2

doughnut shop standbys

TRIED-AND-TRUE CLASSICS YOU GREW UP WITH.

....

Growing up, I remember weekend doughnut trips to Louie's Bakery in Marshall, Michigan, with my dad. My absolute favorites were the glazed buttermilk doughnut holes and the cinnamon powdered sugar doughnut holes. I could never make up my mind on which was best, so the choice was always both. Not surprisingly, these two (page 15 and 30) were the first two doughnuts on my initial list of 101—but you can't go wrong with any one of them!

....

BUTTERMILK DOUGHNUTS
WITH GLAZE OR CHOCOLATE FROSTING

yield: 8 to 10 standard doughnuts

Buttermilk doughnuts. Could anything be more classic? This is an all-time favorite doughnut of mine, which brings back fond childhood memories. This is the closest baked recipe you'll ever find to the real thing.

RECOMMENDED PANS:
Standard, holes

FOR THE DOUGHNUTS:
½ cup (60 g) oat flour
½ cup (70 g) sweet rice flour
⅓ cup (67 g) pure cane sugar
¼ cup (28 g) almond meal
I teaspoon baking powder
½ teaspoon salt
2 large eggs
¼ cup + 3 tablespoons (105 ml) buttermilk
3 tablespoons (45 g) unsweetened applesauce
2 tablespoons (28 ml) oil
2 teaspoons (10 ml) vanilla extract

FOR THE BASIC GLAZE:
I cup (125 g) powdered sugar
2 to 3 tablespoons (30 to 45 ml) milk

FOR THE CHOCOLATE GLAZE:
I cup (120 g) powdered sugar
3 tablespoons (15 g) unsweetened cocoa powder
3 to 4 tablespoons (45 to 60 ml) milk

FOR THE FROSTING:
2 to 3 tablespoons (28 to 45 ml) heavy cream or milk
⅔ cup (80 g) powdered sugar
3 tablespoons (42 g) butter, softened
¼ cup (20 g) unsweetened cocoa powder

TO MAKE THE DOUGHNUTS: Preheat your oven to 350°F (180°C, or gas mark 4) and grease your doughnut pan.

Combine the oat flour, sweet rice flour, cane sugar, almond meal, baking powder, and salt in a large bowl, mixing well. In another bowl, whisk the eggs together. Then add in the buttermilk, applesauce, oil, and vanilla extract. Whisk until well combined. Pour the wet mixture into the dry ingredients and stir with a large wooden spoon until just combined, being careful not to overmix (stop when you no longer see dry flour).

Spoon the batter into the doughnut molds, filling to just below the top of each mold, ⅛- to ¼-inch (3 to 6 mm) from the top. Bake for 18 to 22 minutes until lightly golden brown around the edges. A toothpick inserted in the center should come out clean. Let cool in the pan for 5 minutes. Slide a thin spatula around the edges of the doughnuts to help loosen them out. Then place on a cooling rack and allow to cool fully before icing.

TO MAKE THE BASIC OR CHOCOLATE GLAZE: Mix all the ingredients together with a fork until smooth. Add more milk if a thinner consistency is desired. Invert the doughnut into the glaze, letting the excess drip off, or drizzle the glaze over the doughnut. Let set until the glaze has hardened.

TO MAKE THE FROSTING: Mix the frosting ingredients together until fully combined and smooth. Add more milk if needed.

Spread the chocolate frosting on the doughnuts.

LEMON CURD DOUGHNUTS
WITH TANGY LEMON CURD FILLING

In this doughnut, I've made a tart lemon curd that is stuffed between a sliced lemon-infused doughnut. And if that wasn't enough, you can finish it off with a sweet lemon glaze. In fact, I recommend it. You're going to love the bright and tart flavor that lemon adds to every bite of these doughnuts!

RECOMMENDED PANS:
Standard, mini, twist

FOR THE FILLING:
4 large egg yolks
½ cup (120 ml) lemon juice
⅓ cup (115 g) honey
1½ tablespoons (21 g) butter
1 tablespoon (6 g) lemon zest
2 teaspoons arrowroot starch or
    cornstarch

FOR THE DOUGHNUTS:
½ cup (60 g) oat flour
½ cup (70 g) sweet rice flour
⅓ cup (67 g) pure cane sugar
3 tablespoons (21 g) almond meal
1 teaspoon baking powder
½ teaspoon salt
2 large eggs
⅓ cup (80 ml) milk
¼ cup (60 g) unsweetened applesauce
2 tablespoons (28 ml) oil
2 teaspoons vanilla extract
2 teaspoons lemon zest

FOR THE GLAZE:
¾ cup (90 g) powdered sugar
2 to 3 tablespoons (28 to 45 ml)
    lemon juice

TO MAKE THE FILLING: Whisk filling ingredients together in a pot over medium heat. Bring to a low boil and reduce the heat if needed to keep at a low boil. Whisk frequently for 8 to 12 minutes until you reach a consistency similar to thin pudding. Place in a heat-safe bowl and let cool on the counter for 30 minutes. Place a piece of plastic wrap touching the top of the curd and refrigerate until fully chilled. The mixture will thicken as it chills.

TO MAKE THE DOUGHNUTS: Preheat your oven to 350°F (180°C, or gas mark 4) and grease your doughnut pan.

Combine the oat flour, sweet rice flour, cane sugar, almond meal, baking powder, and salt in a large bowl, mixing well. In another bowl, whisk the eggs together. Then add in the milk, applesauce, oil, vanilla extract, and lemon zest. Whisk until well combined. Pour the wet mixture into the dry ingredients and stir with a large wooden spoon until just combined, being careful not to overmix (stop when you no longer see dry flour).

Spoon the batter into the doughnut molds filling to just below the top of each mold, ⅛- to ¼-inch (3 to 6 mm) from the top. Bake for 18 to 22 minutes until lightly golden around the edges. A toothpick inserted in the center should come out clean. Let cool in the pan for 5 minutes. Slide a thin spatula around the edges of the doughnuts to help loosen them out. Then place on a cooling rack and allow to cool fully before topping.

TO MAKE THE GLAZE: Mix the glaze ingredients together until smooth, adding more lemon juice for a thinner consistency.

Carefully slice each doughnut in half with a small serrated knife. Spread the chilled lemon filling between the two halves. Drizzle with glaze to finish. Serve immediately.

APPLE CIDER DOUGHNUTS
WITH APPLE CIDER GLAZE

yield: 8 to 10 standard doughnuts

This is the epitome of classic fall doughnuts. Apple butter is key in allowing for the tangy and sweet apple flavor to come through in this recipe. With a hint of cinnamon and an apple cider glaze, this doughnut is perfect for dunking in a mug of hot cider.

RECOMMENDED PANS:
Standard, holes, twist

FOR THE DOUGHNUTS:
½ cup (60 g) oat flour
½ cup (70 g) sweet rice flour
¼ cup (28 g) almond meal
¼ cup (50 g) pure cane sugar
I teaspoon baking powder
½ teaspoon salt
½ teaspoon cinnamon
⅛ teaspoon ginger
2 large eggs
⅓ cup (80 ml) no-sugar-added apple cider
3 tablespoons (45 g) unsweetened applesauce
3 tablespoons (45 g) no-sugar-added apple butter
2 tablespoons (28 ml) oil
I½ teaspoons vanilla extract
¼ cup (30 g) peeled and grated apple

FOR THE GLAZE:
I cup (120 g) powdered sugar
2 tablespoons (30 g) apple butter
I to 3 tablespoons (15 to 45 ml) no-sugar-added apple cider

TO MAKE THE DOUGHNUTS: Preheat your oven to 350°F (180°C, or gas mark 4) and grease your doughnut pan.

Combine the oat flour, sweet rice flour, almond meal, cane sugar, baking powder, salt, cinnamon, and ginger in a large bowl, mixing well. In another bowl, whisk the eggs together. Then add the apple cider, applesauce, apple butter, oil, and vanilla extract. Whisk until well combined.

Pour the wet mixture into the dry ingredients and stir with a large wooden spoon until just combined, being careful not to overmix (stop when you no longer see dry flour). Lightly blot the grated apple with a paper towel and then gently fold into the batter.

Spoon the batter into the doughnut molds filling to just below the top of each mold, ⅛- to ¼-inch (3 to 6 mm) from the top. Bake for 18 to 22 minutes until lightly golden brown around the edges. A toothpick inserted in the center should come out clean. Let cool in the pan for 5 minutes. Slide a thin spatula around the edges of the doughnuts to help loosen them out. Then place on a cooling rack and allow to cool fully before topping.

TO MAKE THE GLAZE: Mix the glaze ingredients together until smooth. Add more apple cider if a thinner consistency is desired. Invert the doughnut and dunk it into the glaze, letting the excess drip off. Or, drizzle over the doughnuts. Let set until the glaze has hardened.

CHOCOLATE BUTTERMILK DOUGHNUTS
WITH POWDERED SUGAR

yield: 10 to 12 standard doughnuts

You can top this chocolaty twist on the original buttermilk version with a variety of flavored powdered sugars or coat them in glaze. Or, if you're like me and you can never decide, try one of each!

RECOMMENDED PANS:
Standard, mini, holes, twist

FOR THE DOUGHNUTS:
½ cup (60 g) oat flour
½ cup (70 g) sweet rice flour
½ cup (100 g) pure cane sugar
¼ cup (20 g) unsweetened cocoa
    powder
3 tablespoons (21 g) almond meal
1 teaspoon baking powder
½ teaspoon salt
2 large eggs
½ cup + 2 tablespoons (148 ml)
    buttermilk
¼ cup (60 g) unsweetened
    applesauce
2 tablespoons (28 ml) oil
1 teaspoon vanilla extract

FOR THE PLAIN TOPPING:
1 cup (120 g) powdered sugar

FOR THE CHOCOLATE TOPPING:
1 cup (120 g) powdered sugar
3 tablespoons (15 g) unsweetened
    cocoa powder, sifted

FOR THE CINNAMON TOPPING:
1 cup (120 g) powdered sugar
½ to 1 teaspoon cinnamon

TO MAKE THE DOUGHNUTS: Preheat your oven to 350°F (180°C, or gas mark 4) and grease your doughnut pan.

Combine the oat flour, sweet rice flour, cane sugar, cocoa powder, almond meal, baking powder, and salt in a large bowl, mixing well. In another bowl, whisk the eggs together. Then add in the buttermilk, applesauce, oil, and vanilla extract. Whisk until well combined.

Pour the wet mixture into the dry ingredients and stir with a large wooden spoon until just combined, being careful not to overmix (stop when you no longer see dry flour).

Spoon the batter into the doughnut molds, filling to just below the top of each mold, $1/8$- to ¼-inch (3 to 6 mm) from the top. Bake for 18 to 22 minutes until lightly golden brown around the edges. A toothpick inserted in the center should come out clean. Let cool in the pan for 5 minutes. Slide a thin spatula around the edges of the doughnuts to help loosen them out. Then place on a cooling rack and allow to cool fully before topping.

TO MAKE THE TOPPINGS: If using the plain powdered sugar, sift over the doughnuts and serve.

If using the chocolate powdered sugar, stir the powdered sugar and cocoa powder together until combined. Sift over the doughnuts and serve.

If using the cinnamon powdered sugar, stir the powdered sugar and cinnamon together until combined. Sift over the doughnuts and serve.

MAPLE DOUGHNUT TWISTS
WITH MAPLE GLAZE AND SEA SALT

yield: 8 to 10 standard doughnuts

What is it about maple syrup? And why is it that every time I use maple syrup my hands are sticky all day long? I don't know the answer to either question, but I do know this is on my list of top five favorite doughnuts. Make them now and don't forget the sprinkle of sea salt on top. Trust me!

RECOMMENDED PANS:
Standard, mini, holes, twist

FOR THE DOUGHNUTS:
½ cup (60 g) oat flour
½ cup (70 g) sweet rice flour
3 tablespoons (21 g) almond meal
2 tablespoons (25 g) pure cane sugar
I teaspoon baking powder
½ teaspoon salt
¼ teaspoon cinnamon
2 large eggs
⅓ cup (80 ml) milk
¼ cup (60 g) unsweetened applesauce
3½ tablespoons (70 g) pure maple syrup
2 tablespoons (28 ml) oil
2 teaspoons vanilla extract

FOR THE GLAZE:
I cup (120 g) powdered sugar
¼ cup (80 g) pure maple syrup
I to 3 teaspoons (5 to 15 ml) milk

FOR THE TOPPING:
Large flaked sea salt

TO MAKE THE DOUGHNUTS: Preheat your oven to 350°F (180°C, or gas mark 4) and grease your doughnut pan.

Combine the oat flour, sweet rice flour, almond meal, cane sugar, baking powder, salt, and cinnamon in a large bowl, mixing well. In another bowl, whisk the eggs together. Then add in the milk, applesauce, maple syrup, oil, and vanilla extract. Whisk until well combined.

Pour the wet mixture into the dry ingredients and stir with a large wooden spoon until just combined, being careful not to overmix (stop when you no longer see dry flour).

Spoon the batter into the doughnut molds, filling to just below the top of each mold, $1/8$- to ¼-inch (3 to 6 mm) from the top. Bake for 18 to 22 minutes until lightly golden brown around the edges. A toothpick inserted in the center should come out clean. Let cool in the pan for 5 minutes. Slide a thin spatula around the edges of the doughnuts to help loosen them out. Then place on a cooling rack and allow to cool fully before topping.

TO MAKE THE GLAZE: Mix the glaze ingredients together until smooth. Add more milk if a thinner consistency is desired. Invert the doughnut into the glaze, letting the excess drip off, or drizzle the glaze over the doughnut. Top with a sprinkle of sea salt. Let set until the glaze has hardened.

HONEY DIP DOUGHNUTS
WITH HONEY GLAZE

yield: 8 to 10 standard doughnuts

You may be thinking that dipping a doughnut in honey will create a hugely sticky mess. However, dipping a doughnut in just-boiled honey makes it a bit easier. The honey becomes runny after boiling and soaks into the doughnut without making it soggy or overly sticky. These doughnuts are sweet, cakey, and addictive—watch out.

RECOMMENDED PANS:
Standard, mini, holes, twist

FOR THE DOUGHNUTS:
½ cup (60 g) oat flour
½ cup (70 g) sweet rice flour
3 tablespoons (21 g) almond meal
2 tablespoons (25 g) pure cane sugar
1 teaspoon baking powder
½ teaspoon salt
2 large eggs
¼ cup + 2 tablespoons (88 ml) buttermilk
¼ cup (60 g) unsweetened applesauce
3 tablespoons (60 g) honey
2 tablespoons (28 ml) oil
1 teaspoon vanilla extract

FOR THE TOPPING:
1 cup (340 g) honey

TO MAKE THE DOUGHNUTS: Preheat your oven to 350°F (180°C, or gas mark 4) and grease your doughnut pan.

Combine the oat flour, sweet rice flour, almond meal, cane sugar, baking powder, and salt in a large bowl, mixing well. In another bowl, whisk the eggs together. Then add the buttermilk, apple-sauce, honey, oil, and vanilla extract. Whisk until well combined.

Pour the wet mixture into the dry ingredients and stir with a large wooden spoon until just combined, being careful not to overmix (stop when you no longer see dry flour).

Spoon the batter into the doughnut molds, filling to just below the top of each mold, $1/8$- to ¼-inch (3 to 6 mm) from the top. Bake for 18 to 22 minutes until lightly golden brown around the edges. A toothpick inserted in the center should come out clean. Let cool in the pan for 5 minutes. Slide a thin spatula around the edges of the doughnuts to help loosen them out. Then place on a cooling rack and allow to cool fully before topping.

TO MAKE THE TOPPING: In a small pot over medium-low heat, bring the honey to a low boil, whisking constantly. Turn off the heat and pour in a shallow bowl, just large enough to dip the doughnuts. Very carefully (honey will be very hot!) dip the top of the doughnut in the honey and let the excess drip off.

Place on a cooling rack and serve once cooled.

APPLE FRITTER DOUGHNUTS
WITH CRISPY CINNAMON-SUGAR COATING

yield: 8 to 10 standard doughnuts

While you may be thinking an apple fritter just *has* to be fried, you will definitely think otherwise after trying this recipe. Brushing the doughnuts with butter, coating them with cinnamon-sugar, and placing them under the broiler is the trick to achieving a crunchy fried-like outer shell, making them the closest thing to a fried doughnut you will ever create without actually pulling out a fryer. They firm when cooled and remind me of the elephant ears I used to obsess over at summer carnivals growing up—so good!

RECOMMENDED PANS:
Standard, holes

FOR THE DOUGHNUTS:
½ cup (60 g) oat flour
½ cup (70 g) sweet rice flour
⅓ cup (67 g) pure cane sugar
3 tablespoons (21 g) almond meal
1 teaspoon baking powder
1 teaspoon cinnamon
½ teaspoon salt
2 large eggs
¼ cup + 2 tablespoons (88 ml) buttermilk
¼ cup (60 g) unsweetened applesauce
2 tablespoons (28 ml) oil
1½ teaspoons vanilla extract
½ cup (75 g) peeled and diced apple

FOR THE TOPPING:
¾ cup (150 g) pure cane sugar
¾ teaspoon cinnamon
¼ cup (55 g) butter, melted

TO MAKE THE DOUGHNUTS: Preheat your oven to 350°F (180°C, or gas mark 4) and grease your doughnut pan.

Combine the oat flour, sweet rice flour, cane sugar, almond meal, baking powder, cinnamon, and salt in a large bowl, mixing well. In another bowl, whisk the eggs together. Then add the buttermilk, applesauce, oil, and vanilla extract. Whisk until well combined.

Pour the wet mixture into the dry ingredients and stir with a large wooden spoon until just combined, being careful not to overmix (stop when you no longer see dry flour). Gently fold the diced apple into the batter.

Spoon the batter into the doughnut molds filling to just below the top of each mold, ⅛- to ¼-inch (3 to 6 mm) from the top. Bake for 18 to 22 minutes until lightly golden brown around the edges. A toothpick inserted in the center should come out clean. Let cool in the pan for 5 minutes. Slide a thin spatula around the edges of the doughnuts to help loosen them out. Then place on a cooling rack and allow to cool fully before topping.

TO MAKE THE TOPPING: Preheat your oven to broil over low heat and place a rack at the top position. Place an oven-safe wire rack on a rimmed baking sheet.

Mix the cane sugar and cinnamon in a bowl. Brush the doughnuts on all sides with the butter and coat fully with the cinnamon-sugar mixture.

Place each doughnut on the wire rack and then place under the broiler, watching closely, for 1 to 3 minutes until the sugar starts to bubble and melt. Remove from the oven and gently flip over (the doughnuts will be soft and fragile while hot). Broil again for another 1 to 3 minutes and then remove from the oven. As the doughnuts cool, they will firm and form a crunchy outer coating.

JELLY-FILLED DOUGHNUTS
WITH POWDERED SUGAR

yield: 8 to 10 standard doughnuts

I was really unsure if this doughnut would work or not. I thought the jelly would soak into the doughnut when baked. But to my surprise, it didn't. When you bite into the doughnut, you'll find a fruity, jelly center. Now as to whether you should fill it with strawberry or grape jelly, I will leave up to you.

RECOMMENDED PANS:
Standard, holes, twist

FOR THE DOUGHNUTS:
½ cup (60 g) oat flour
½ cup (70 g) sweet rice flour
⅓ cup (67 g) pure cane sugar
3 tablespoons (21 g) almond meal
I teaspoon baking powder
½ teaspoon salt
2 large eggs
¼ cup + 2 tablespoons (88 ml) buttermilk
¼ cup (60 g) unsweetened
    applesauce
2 tablespoons (28 ml) oil
1½ teaspoons vanilla extract
6 tablespoons (108 g) fruit juice–
    sweetened jelly

FOR THE TOPPING:
I cup (120 g) powdered sugar

Preheat your oven to 350°F (180°C, or gas mark 4) and grease your doughnut pan.

Combine the oat flour, sweet rice flour, cane sugar, almond meal, baking powder, and salt in a large bowl, mixing well. In another bowl, whisk the eggs together. Then add the buttermilk, applesauce, oil, and vanilla extract. Whisk until well combined.

Pour the wet mixture into the dry ingredients and stir with a large wooden spoon until just combined, being careful not to overmix (stop when you no longer see dry flour).

Spoon the batter into the doughnut molds, filling only halfway. Dot about 2 teaspoons (10 g) of jelly going around the centerline of each doughnut. Fill the molds with the remaining batter just below the top of each mold, $1/8$- to ¼-inch (3 to 6 mm) from the top.

Bake for 18 to 22 minutes until lightly golden brown around the edges. A toothpick inserted in the center should come out clean. Let cool in the pan for 5 minutes. Slide a thin spatula around the edges of the doughnuts to help loosen them out. Then place on a cooling rack and allow to cool fully before topping. Sift powdered sugar over each doughnut to finish.

BOSTON CREAM DOUGHNUTS
WITH VANILLA FILLING AND CHOCOLATE GANACHE

yield: 6 to 8 standard doughnuts

Did you ever think you'd be making a Boston cream doughnut in the comfort of your home? You'll never have to step inside a doughnut shop again!

RECOMMENDED PANS:
Standard, twist

FOR THE FILLING:
1¼ cups (300 ml) 2% milk
¼ cup (60 ml) half-and-half
¼ cup (50 g) pure cane sugar
1½ tablespoons (12 g) arrowroot starch
 or cornstarch
1 large egg
1 large egg yolk
⅛ teaspoon salt
½ scraped vanilla bean and pod

FOR THE TOPPING:
1 cup (175 g) dark chocolate chips
4 to 6 tablespoons (60 to 90 ml)
 heavy cream

FOR THE DOUGHNUTS:
½ cup (60 g) oat flour
½ cup (70 g) sweet rice flour
3 tablespoons (21 g) almond meal
⅓ cup (67 g) pure cane sugar
1 teaspoon baking powder
½ teaspoon salt
2 large eggs
⅓ cup (80 ml) milk
¼ cup (50 g) plain Greek yogurt
2 tablespoons (28 ml) oil
2 teaspoons vanilla extract

TO MAKE THE FILLING: Place a fine-mesh strainer over a large bowl. Whisk the milk, half-and-half, cane sugar, arrowroot starch, eggs, salt, and vanilla beans in a pot until smooth. Place the half scraped vanilla bean pod in the pot. Heat over medium-high heat until simmering, whisking constantly. After a simmer is reached, stir and simmer for 1 minute. Then turn off the heat and pour the mixture through the strainer. Discard the vanilla bean pod.

Place in a heat-safe bowl and let sit for 30 minutes. Place a piece of plastic wrap touching the filling and refrigerate until fully chilled. The mixture will thicken and should be the consistency of pudding.

TO MAKE THE TOPPING: Melt the chocolate with ¼ cup (60 ml) heavy cream using a double boiler, stirring until smooth. Add more heavy cream to thin out and stir until smooth. Remove from heat. Place in a bowl to let cool to room temperature. The mixture will thicken as it cools.

TO MAKE THE DOUGHNUTS: Preheat your oven to 350°F (180°C, or gas mark 4) and grease your doughnut pan.

Combine the dry doughnut ingredients in a large bowl, mixing well. In another bowl, whisk the eggs together. Then add the milk, yogurt, oil, and vanilla extract. Whisk until well combined.

Pour the wet mixture into the dry ingredients and stir with a large wooden spoon until just combined, being careful not to overmix (stop when you no longer see dry flour).

Spoon the batter into the doughnut molds, filling to just below the top of each mold, ⅛- to ¼-inch (3 to 6 mm) from the top. Bake for 18 to 22 minutes until lightly golden brown around the edges. A toothpick inserted in the center should come out clean. Let cool in the pan for 5 minutes. Slide a thin spatula around the edges to help loosen them out. Then place on a cooling rack and allow to cool fully before topping.

Slice each doughnut in half with a small serrated knife. Spread the filling on the bottom half. Spread a coating of ganache on the top half and sandwich together. Serve immediately.

CINNAMON CAKE DOUGHNUTS
WITH CINNAMON-SUGAR COATING

yield: 6 to 8 standard doughnuts

Hi. My name is Ashley and I have an addiction to cinnamon. What's that? You do too? Perfect. We'll be best friends. When you come, over I'll make you these doughnuts. They're infused with cinnamon and then topped with even more. They're a cinnamon explosion. Sound good?

RECOMMENDED PANS:
Standard, mini, holes, twist

FOR THE DOUGHNUTS:
½ cup (60 g) oat flour
½ cup (70 g) sweet rice flour
⅓ cup (67 g) pure cane sugar
3 tablespoons (21 g) almond meal
2 teaspoons cinnamon
1 teaspoon baking powder
½ teaspoon salt
2 large eggs
½ cup (120 ml) buttermilk
¼ cup (60 g) unsweetened applesauce
2 tablespoons (28 ml) oil
2 teaspoons vanilla extract

FOR THE TOPPING:
½ cup (100 g) pure cane sugar
½ teaspoon cinnamon
4 tablespoons (55 g) butter, melted

TO MAKE THE DOUGHNUTS: Preheat your oven to 350°F (180°C, or gas mark 4) and grease your doughnut pan.

Combine the oat flour, sweet rice flour, cane sugar, almond meal, cinnamon, baking powder, and salt in a large bowl, mixing well. In another bowl, whisk the eggs together. Then add in the buttermilk, applesauce, oil, and vanilla extract. Whisk until well combined.

Pour the wet mixture into the dry ingredients and stir with a large wooden spoon until just combined, being careful not to overmix (stop when you no longer see dry flour).

Spoon the batter into the doughnut molds, filling to just below the top of each mold, ⅛- to ¼-inch (3 to 6 mm) from the top. Bake for 18 to 22 minutes until lightly golden brown around the edges. A toothpick inserted in the center should come out clean. Let cool in the pan for 5 minutes. Slide a thin spatula around the edges of the doughnuts to help loosen them out. Then place on a cooling rack and allow to cool fully before topping.

TO MAKE THE TOPPING: Mix the sugar and cinnamon together in a bowl. Brush melted butter on all sides of the doughnuts, sprinkle with (or dip into) the cinnamon-sugar, and serve.

BLUEBERRY GLAZED DOUGHNUTS
WITH CRUMB TOPPING

yield: 8 to 10 standard doughnuts

If there were ever a doughnut fit for breakfast this would be it! I've taken the classic blueberry glazed doughnut and jazzed it up a bit with an oat crumb topping. It gives it that little extra somethin' somethin'. Serve with a mug of hot coffee and you're all set!

RECOMMENDED PANS:
Standard, mini, holes, twist

FOR THE DOUGHNUTS:
½ cup (60 g) oat flour
½ cup (70 g) sweet rice flour
⅓ cup (67 g) pure cane sugar
¼ cup (28 g) almond meal
1 teaspoon baking powder
½ teaspoon salt
2 large eggs
¼ cup + 2 tablespoons (88 ml) milk
3 tablespoons (45 g) unsweetened
    applesauce
2 tablespoons (28 ml) oil
1½ teaspoons vanilla extract
¼ cup + 2 tablespoons (54 g) fresh
    blueberries

FOR THE TOPPING:
2 tablespoons (28 g) butter
½ cup (40 g) rolled oats
3 tablespoons (45 g) packed brown
    sugar
Fresh blueberries

FOR THE GLAZE:
1 cup (120 g) powdered sugar
3 tablespoons (45 ml) milk

TO MAKE THE DOUGHNUTS: Preheat your oven to 350°F (180°C, or gas mark 4) and grease your doughnut pan.

Combine the oat flour, sweet rice flour, cane sugar, almond meal, baking powder, and salt in a large bowl, mixing well. In another bowl, whisk the eggs together. Then add in the milk, applesauce, oil, and vanilla extract. Whisk until well combined.

Pour the wet mixture into the dry ingredients and stir with a large wooden spoon until just combined, being careful not to overmix (stop when you no longer see dry flour). Gently fold the blueberries into the batter.

Spoon the batter into the doughnut molds, filling to just below the top of each mold, ⅛- to ¼-inch (3 to 6 mm) from the top. Bake for 20 to 24 minutes until lightly golden brown around the edges. A toothpick inserted in the center should come out clean. Let cool in the pan for 5 minutes. Slide a thin spatula around the edges of the doughnuts to help loosen them out. Then place on a cooling rack and allow to cool fully before topping.

TO MAKE THE TOPPING: Melt the butter in a small pan over medium heat. Once melted, add in the oats and brown sugar. Cook for 4 to 6 minutes until the oats start to turn light golden brown, stirring frequently during cooking to avoid burning the sugar. Let cool.

TO MAKE THE GLAZE: Combine the glaze ingredients in a small bowl and mix well. The glaze will be very thin. Invert the doughnut into the glaze and let the excess drip off.

Sprinkle the oat crumb topping and fresh blueberries over top and let set until the glaze has hardened.

HONEY NUT ROLL DOUGHNUTS
WITH HONEY PECAN TOPPING

●●●●●●●●●●●●●●●●●●●● *yield: 8 to 10 standard doughnuts* ●●●●●●●●●●●●●●●●●

When it comes to roasted nuts, pecans are where it's at. I adore making this doughnut in twist form to take on the idea of the traditional nut roll. The tops are dipped in honey and then covered in roasted pecans, which lend a nutty, buttery flavor. Pecan lovers unite!

RECOMMENDED PANS:
Standard, mini, holes, twist

FOR THE DOUGHNUTS:
½ cup (60 g) oat flour
½ cup (70 g) sweet rice flour
¼ cup (28 g) pecan meal
2 tablespoons (25 g) pure cane sugar
I teaspoon baking powder
½ teaspoon salt
¼ teaspoon cinnamon
2 large eggs
⅓ cup (80 ml) milk
¼ cup (60 g) unsweetened applesauce
3 tablespoons (60 g) honey
2 tablespoons (28 ml) oil
I½ teaspoons vanilla extract

FOR THE TOPPING:
½ cup (170 g) honey
I cup (110 g) toasted chopped pecans

TO MAKE THE DOUGHNUTS: Preheat your oven to 350°F (180°C, or gas mark 4) and grease your doughnut pan.

Combine the oat flour, sweet rice flour, pecan meal, cane sugar, baking powder, salt, and cinnamon in a large bowl, mixing well. In another bowl, whisk the eggs together. Then add in the milk, applesauce, honey, oil, and vanilla extract. Whisk until well combined.

Pour the wet mixture into the dry ingredients and stir with a large wooden spoon until just combined, being careful not to overmix (stop when you no longer see dry flour).

Spoon the batter into the doughnut molds, filling to just below the top of each mold, ⅛- to ¼-inch (3 to 6 mm) from the top. Bake for 18 to 22 minutes until lightly golden brown around the edges. A toothpick inserted in the center should come out clean. Let cool in the pan for 5 minutes. Slide a thin spatula around the edges of the doughnuts to help loosen them out. Then place on a cooling rack and allow to cool fully before topping.

TO MAKE THE TOPPING: In a small pot over medium-low heat, bring the honey to a low boil, whisking constantly. Turn off the heat and pour in a shallow bowl, just large enough to dip the doughnuts. Very carefully (honey will be very hot!) dip the top of the doughnut in the honey and let the excess drip off.

Place on a cooling rack and top with toasted pecans. Let cool for 15 to 20 minutes before serving.

CHAPTER 3

fruit-filled treats

FRUIT AND DOUGHNUTS TOGETHER? YOU'LL BE GLAD YOU DID.

With the popularity of fruit-filled muffins, pancakes, and the like, I figured why not add doughnuts to the list? Here you will find a wide variety of recipes that are filled to the brim with fresh fruit. From the doughnuts themselves, to the glazes and frostings, fruit is the key to this chapter!

BLUEBERRY LEMON CAKE DOUGHNUTS
WITH TANGY LEMON GLAZE

● *yield: 8 to 10 standard doughnuts*

Blueberry and lemon is a favorite flavor combination of mine. The blueberries give a burst of juice while the lemon brightens each bite. The glaze is sweet and slightly mouth puckering. I like to think of this as the perfect Sunday doughnut.

RECOMMENDED PANS:
Standard, mini, holes, twist

FOR THE DOUGHNUTS:
½ cup (60 g) oat flour
½ cup (70 g) sweet rice flour
⅓ cup (67 g) pure cane sugar
¼ cup (28 g) almond meal
I teaspoon baking powder
½ teaspoon salt
2 large eggs
⅓ cup (80 ml) unsweetened almond milk
3 tablespoons (45 g) unsweetened
   applesauce
2 tablespoons (28 ml) oil
I tablespoon (6 g) lemon zest
2 teaspoons lemon juice
I½ teaspoons vanilla extract
½ cup (75 g) blueberries

FOR THE GLAZE:
I cup (120 g) powdered sugar
I to 2 tablespoons (15 to 28 ml) milk
I tablespoon (15 ml) lemon juice
I teaspoon lemon zest

TO MAKE THE DOUGHNUTS: Preheat your oven to 350°F (180°C, or gas mark 4) and grease your doughnut pan.

Combine the oat flour, sweet rice flour, cane sugar, almond meal, baking powder, and salt in a large bowl, mixing well. In another bowl, whisk the eggs together. Then add in the milk, applesauce, oil, lemon zest, lemon juice, and vanilla extract. Whisk until well combined.

Pour the wet mixture into the dry ingredients and stir with a large wooden spoon until just combined, being careful not to overmix (stop when you no longer see dry flour). Gently fold the blueberries into the batter.

Spoon the batter into the doughnut molds, filling to just below the top of each mold, ⅛- to ¼-inch (3 to 6 mm) from the top. Bake for 20 to 24 minutes until lightly golden brown around the edges. A toothpick inserted in the center should come out clean. Let cool in the pan for 5 minutes. Slide a thin spatula around the edges of the doughnuts to help loosen them out. Then place on a cooling rack and allow to cool fully before icing.

TO MAKE THE GLAZE: Mix the ingredients together until smooth. Add more milk if a thinner consistency is desired. Invert the doughnut into the glaze, letting the excess drip off, or drizzle the glaze over the doughnut. Let rest until the glaze has hardened.

RASPBERRY WHITE CHOCOLATE DOUGHNUTS
WITH WHITE CHOCOLATE SHELL AND RASPBERRIES

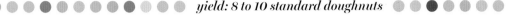

yield: 8 to 10 standard doughnuts

Creamy white chocolate and juicy, sweet raspberries hit you with every bite in this next doughnut creation. The crunchy shell topping is the perfect contrast to this fresh, cakey doughnut. If white chocolate is not your thing, use dark chocolate instead!

RECOMMENDED PANS:
Standard, holes

FOR THE DOUGHNUTS:
½ cup (60 g) oat flour
½ cup (70 g) sweet rice flour
¼ cup (28 g) almond meal
¼ cup (50 g) pure cane sugar
I teaspoon baking powder
½ teaspoon salt
2 large eggs
¼ cup + 2 tablespoons (88 ml) milk
3 tablespoons (45 g) unsweetened
   applesauce
2 tablespoons (28 ml) oil
1½ teaspoons vanilla extract
⅓ cup (58 g) chopped white chocolate
   chips
⅓ cup (42 g) chopped fresh
   raspberries

FOR THE TOPPING:
I cup (175 g) white chocolate chips
Fresh raspberries, halved

TO MAKE THE DOUGHNUTS: Preheat your oven to 350°F (180°C, or gas mark 4) and grease your doughnut pan.

Combine the oat flour, sweet rice flour, almond meal, cane sugar, baking powder, and salt in a large bowl, mixing well. In another bowl, whisk the eggs together. Then add in the milk, applesauce, oil, and vanilla extract. Whisk until well combined.

Pour the wet mixture into the dry ingredients and stir with a large wooden spoon until just combined, being careful not to overmix (stop when you no longer see dry flour). Lightly blot the chopped raspberries with a paper towel and gently fold them, along with the white chocolate, into the batter.

Spoon the batter into the doughnut molds filling to just below the top of each mold, ⅛- to ¼-inch (3 to 6 mm) from the top. Bake for 20 to 24 minutes until lightly golden brown around the edges. A toothpick inserted in the center should come out clean. Let cool in the pan for 5 minutes. Slide a thin spatula around the edges of the doughnuts to help loosen them out. Then place on a cooling rack and allow to cool fully before topping.

TO MAKE THE TOPPING: Melt the white chocolate in a double boiler, stirring until smooth, or place the chocolate in a small microwave-safe bowl and microwave for 30-second increments, stirring after each interval, until the white chocolate is smooth.

Invert the doughnut into the melted chocolate and let the excess drip off. Top with halved raspberries (blot dry if they are wet) and let set until the chocolate has hardened.

CHERRY ALMOND DOUGHNUTS
WITH CHERRY ALMOND ICING

yield: 8 to 10 standard doughnuts

An all-time favorite flavor combination, these doughnuts are studded with sweet cherries throughout. The vibrant pink icing is naturally dyed with cherry juice and the cake has a distinct almond aroma. Top with a sprinkle of crunchy, toasted almonds and they are ready for you to enjoy.

RECOMMENDED PANS:
Standard, holes

FOR THE DOUGHNUTS:
½ cup (60 g) oat flour
½ cup (70 g) sweet rice flour
⅓ cup (67 g) pure cane sugar
¼ cup (28 g) almond meal
I teaspoon baking powder
½ teaspoon salt
2 large eggs
¼ cup + 2 tablespoons (88 ml) milk
3 tablespoons (45 g) unsweetened
   applesauce
2 tablespoons (28 ml) oil
1½ teaspoons vanilla extract
½ teaspoon almond extract
⅓ cup (52 g) chopped bing
   cherries

FOR THE TOPPING:
½ cup (46 g) sliced almonds

FOR THE ICING:
8 to 12 whole bing cherries, pitted
I cup (120 g) powdered sugar
1½ tablespoons (21 g) butter, softened
¼ teaspoon almond extract

TO MAKE THE DOUGHNUTS: Preheat your oven to 350°F (180°C, or gas mark 4) and grease your doughnut pan.

Combine the oat flour, sweet rice flour, cane sugar, almond meal, baking powder, and salt in a large bowl, mixing well. In another bowl, whisk the eggs together. Then add in the milk, applesauce, oil, vanilla extract, and almond extract. Whisk well. Pour the wet mixture into the dry ingredients and stir with a large wooden spoon until just combined, being careful not to overmix (stop when you no longer see dry flour). Blot the chopped cherries with a paper towel and gently fold them into the batter.

Spoon the batter into the doughnut molds, filling to just below the top of each mold, $1/8$- to ¼-inch (3 to 6 mm) from the top. Bake for 20 to 24 minutes until lightly golden brown around the edges. A toothpick inserted in the center should come out clean. Let cool in the pan for 5 minutes. Slide a thin spatula around the edges of the doughnuts to help loosen them out. Then place on a cooling rack and allow to cool fully before icing.

TO MAKE THE TOPPING: Heat a small pan over medium-low heat. Add the sliced almonds and toast for 5 to 8 minutes, stirring frequently, until light golden brown in color. Remove from the heat and let cool.

TO MAKE THE ICING: Place the pitted cherries in a fine-mesh strainer over a bowl and press with the back of a fork until you've extracted about 2 tablespoons (28 ml) of juice into the bowl. Discard the skins. Add the remaining icing ingredients to the juice in the bowl. Mix until the ingredients are smooth. Add more cherry juice if a thinner icing is desired.

Drizzle or spread icing on the cooled doughnuts. Sprinkle with sliced almonds and let the doughnuts set until the icing has hardened.

BLACKBERRY BASIL DOUGHNUTS
WITH BLACKBERRY ICING

●●●●●●●●●●●●●●●● *yield: 8 to 10 standard doughnuts* ●●●●●●●●●●●●●●●●

This doughnut might raise an eyebrow, but I assure you it's quite a common flavor combination. I've seen blackberry basil grilled cheese sandwiches, blackberry basil cocktails and smoothies, blackberry basil ice cream, and many other recipes utilizing these two ingredients. Now you can enjoy this adventurous variety in a baked doughnut!

RECOMMENDED PANS:
Standard, holes

FOR THE DOUGHNUTS:
½ cup (60 g) oat flour
½ cup (70 g) sweet rice flour
⅓ cup (67 g) pure cane sugar
¼ cup (28 g) almond meal
1 teaspoon baking powder
½ teaspoon salt
2 large eggs
¼ cup + 2 tablespoons (88 ml) milk
3 tablespoons (45 g) unsweetened
　applesauce
2 tablespoons (28 ml) oil
1½ teaspoons vanilla extract
⅓ cup (48 g) chopped fresh blackberries
3 tablespoons (8 g) finely chopped basil

FOR THE ICING:
10 whole blackberries
1 cup (120 g) powdered sugar
1 tablespoon (14 g) butter, softened

TO MAKE THE DOUGHNUTS: Preheat your oven to 350°F (180°C, or gas mark 4) and grease your doughnut pan.

Combine the oat flour, sweet rice flour, cane sugar, almond meal, baking powder, and salt in a large bowl, mixing well. In another bowl, whisk the eggs together. Then add in the milk, applesauce, oil, and vanilla extract. Whisk until well combined.

Pour the wet mixture into the dry ingredients and stir with a large wooden spoon until just combined, being careful not to overmix (stop when you no longer see dry flour). Lightly blot the chopped blackberries with a paper towel and gently fold them, along with the basil, into the batter.

Spoon the batter into the doughnut molds, filling to just below the top of each mold, ⅛- to ¼-inch (3 to 6 mm) from the top. Bake for 20 to 24 minutes until lightly golden brown around the edges. A toothpick inserted in the center should come out clean. Let cool in the pan for 5 minutes. Slide a thin spatula around the edges of the doughnuts to help loosen them out. Then place on a cooling rack and allow to cool fully before icing.

TO MAKE THE ICING: Mash about 10 blackberries in a bowl until completely broken apart and measure out 3 tablespoons (45 g) worth. Add the remaining icing ingredients and mix with a fork until thoroughly combined. Add strained blackberry juice if a thinner icing is desired. Spread onto the doughnuts and let set until the icing has hardened.

RECIPE NOTE

If you don't want seeds in the glaze, mash the blackberries in a fine-mesh strainer set over a bowl to collect the juice. Start by adding 1 tablespoon (15 ml) of blackberry juice to the other icing ingredients and add more until your desired consistency is met.

VEGAN BLOOD ORANGE DOUGHNUTS
WITH CHOCOLATE GLAZE AND BLOOD ORANGE DRIZZLE

yield: 8 to 10 standard doughnuts

This vegan doughnut is livened up with the addition of vibrant blood orange juice and zest. It's then drenched in a thick chocolate glaze and finished with a pink-hued blood orange drizzle.

RECOMMENDED PANS:
Standard

FOR THE DOUGHNUTS:
½ cup (60 g) oat flour
½ cup (70 g) sweet rice flour
⅓ cup (67 g) pure cane sugar
2 tablespoons (14 g) almond meal
2 tablespoons (14 g) coconut flour
2 tablespoons (14 g) ground flax meal
1 teaspoon baking powder
½ teaspoon baking soda
½ teaspoon salt
¼ cup + 2 tablespoons (88 ml) blood
    orange juice, freshly squeezed
¼ cup (60 ml) nondairy milk
3 tablespoons (45 g) unsweetened
    applesauce
3 tablespoons (45 ml) oil
1 tablespoon (6 g) blood orange zest
1½ teaspoons vanilla extract

FOR THE GLAZE:
1 cup (120 g) powdered sugar
4 to 6 tablespoons (60 to 90 ml)
    nondairy milk
3 tablespoons (15 g) unsweetened cocoa
    powder

FOR THE DRIZZLE:
¼ cup (30 g) powdered sugar
2 to 3 teaspoons (10 to 15 ml) blood
    orange juice, freshly squeezed

TO MAKE THE DOUGHNUTS: Preheat your oven to 350°F (180°C, or gas mark 4) and grease your doughnut pan.

Combine the oat flour, sweet rice flour, cane sugar, almond meal, coconut flour, ground flax, baking powder, baking soda, and salt in a large bowl, mixing well. In another bowl, whisk together the orange juice, nondairy milk, applesauce, oil, orange zest, and vanilla extract until well combined.

Pour the wet mixture into the dry ingredients and stir with a large wooden spoon until just combined, being careful not to overmix (stop when you no longer see dry flour). Let sit for 5 minutes and do not stir after this point. The batter will be very thick and not pourable.

Spoon the batter into the doughnut molds, filling to just below the top of each mold, ⅛- to ¼-inch (3 to 6 mm) from the top. Lightly even out the top of the batter with a small silicone spatula. Do not press down on the batter. Bake for 18 to 22 minutes until lightly golden brown around the edges. A toothpick inserted in the center should come out clean. Let cool in the pan for 5 minutes. Slide a thin spatula around the edges of the doughnuts to help loosen them out. Then place on a cooling rack and allow to cool fully before topping.

TO MAKE THE GLAZE: Mix the glaze ingredients together until smooth. Add more nondairy milk for a thinner consistency.

Invert doughnuts into the coating and let the excess drip off. Let set until glaze has hardened and then apply drizzle.

TO MAKE THE DRIZZLE: Mix the drizzle ingredients together until smooth. You want a very thick consistency. Pour into a sealable plastic bag and cut a tiny opening in one corner. Gently squeeze out over the doughnuts in a zigzag pattern.

HONEY LEMON RHUBARB DOUGHNUTS
WITH TANGY RHUBARB GLAZE

yield: 8 to 10 standard doughnuts

My grandpa was the only person I ever knew who ate rhubarb, and it was only ever in pie. I'm not sure what took me so long to try it, but I just love this unique vegetable. The rhubarb lemon glaze lends a tart taste to this doughnut that might make your mouth do a double take.

RECOMMENDED PANS:
Standard, mini, holes

FOR THE RHUBARB PURÉE:
2 cups (244 g) chopped rhubarb
2 tablespoons (40 g) honey
I teaspoon sweet rice flour

FOR THE DOUGHNUTS:
½ cup (60 g) oat flour
½ cup (70 g) sweet rice flour
⅓ cup (67 g) pure cane sugar
3 tablespoons (21 g) almond meal
I teaspoon baking powder
½ teaspoon salt
2 large eggs
⅓ cup (80 ml) milk
⅓ cup (85 g) rhubarb purée
3 tablespoons (45 g) unsweetened
    applesauce
2 tablespoons (28 ml) oil
2 teaspoons lemon zest
I½ teaspoons vanilla extract

FOR THE GLAZE:
⅔ cup (170 g) rhubarb purée
¼ to ⅓ (30 to 40 g) cup powdered sugar

FOR THE TOPPING:
Lemon zest

TO MAKE THE PURÉE: Place rhubarb, honey, and flour in a pan over medium heat and stir together. Bring to a low boil, stirring frequently. Reduce the heat to simmer and stir occasionally for 10 to 15 minutes until the rhubarb is broken down and thickened. Let cool for at least 5 minutes and then place in your blender and purée. Let cool fully.

TO MAKE THE DOUGHNUTS: Preheat your oven to 350°F (180°C, or gas mark 4) and grease your doughnut pan.

Combine the oat flour, sweet rice flour, cane sugar, almond meal, baking powder, and salt in a large bowl, mixing well. In another bowl, whisk the eggs together. Then add in the milk, rhubarb purée, applesauce, oil, lemon zest, and vanilla extract. Whisk until well combined.

Pour the wet mixture into the dry ingredients and stir with a large wooden spoon until just combined, being careful not to overmix (stop when you no longer see dry flour).

Spoon the batter into the doughnut molds, filling to just below the top of each mold, ⅛- to ¼-inch (3 to 6 mm) from the top. Bake for 18 to 22 minutes until lightly golden brown around the edges. A toothpick inserted in the center should come out clean. Let cool in the pan for 5 minutes. Slide a thin spatula around the edges of the doughnuts to help loosen them out. Then place on a cooling rack and allow to cool fully before topping.

TO MAKE THE GLAZE: Mix the cooled purée and powdered sugar together until smooth. Spread over the doughnuts with a small spatula, top with lemon zest, and serve immediately. The glaze will not set.

DRIED FIG AND GOAT CHEESE DOUGHNUTS
WITH SWEET GOAT CHEESE ICING

yield: 8 to 10 standard doughnuts

If you like the flavor of figs in the classic Fig Newton cookie, then these are a must-try! Sweet meets tangy in this unique doughnut pairing. The silky smooth goat cheese has just enough of a pop to balance out the natural sweetness of the dried figs.

RECOMMENDED PANS:
Standard, holes

FOR THE DOUGHNUTS:
½ cup (60 g) oat flour
½ cup (70 g) sweet rice flour
⅓ cup (67 g) pure cane sugar
3 tablespoons (21 g) almond meal
1 teaspoon baking powder
½ teaspoon salt
2 large eggs
¼ cup + 2 tablespoons (88 ml) milk
¼ cup (60 g) unsweetened applesauce
2 tablespoons (28 ml) oil
1½ teaspoons vanilla extract
⅓ cup (50 g) crumbled goat cheese, softened
½ cup (75 g) chopped dried figs, de-stemmed

FOR THE ICING:
1 cup (120 g) powdered sugar
1 tablespoon (15 ml) milk
1½ tablespoons (14 g) goat cheese, softened

FOR THE TOPPING:
Dried figs, chopped and de-stemmed

TO MAKE THE DOUGHNUTS: Preheat your oven to 350°F (180°C, or gas mark 4) and grease your doughnut pan.

Combine the oat flour, sweet rice flour, cane sugar, almond meal, baking powder, and salt in a large bowl, mixing well. In another bowl, whisk the eggs together. Then add in the milk, applesauce, oil, and vanilla extract. Whisk until well combined. Vigorously whisk in the goat cheese until it's broken apart and evenly distributed. The mixture will not be fully smooth.

Pour the wet mixture into the dry ingredients and stir with a large wooden spoon until just combined, being careful not to overmix (stop when you no longer see dry flour). Gently fold in the dried figs.

Spoon the batter into the doughnut molds, filling to just below the top of each mold, ⅛- to ¼-inch (3 to 6 mm) from the top. Bake for 20 to 24 minutes until lightly golden brown around the edges. A toothpick inserted in the center should come out clean. Let cool in the pan for 5 minutes. Slide a thin spatula around the edges of the doughnuts to help loosen them out. Then place on a cooling rack and allow to cool fully before icing.

TO MAKE THE ICING: Combine all of the icing ingredients in a small bowl and mix until smooth. Slowly add more milk if a thinner icing is desired. Spread onto the doughnuts, top with chopped dried figs, and let set until the icing has hardened.

STRAWBERRY CHEESECAKE DOUGHNUTS
WITH LEMON FROSTING, STRAWBERRIES, AND GRAHAM CRACKERS

yield: 8 to 10 standard doughnuts

Perfect for a Sunday brunch, a baby shower, or any sunny-summery day, this doughnut will keep you coming back for more. Seriously. You won't be able to stop eating them. It starts with the fluffy dough-nut, then moves to the lemony cheesecake creaminess, and ends with a burst of juice from the straw-berries. A cheesecake doughnut? Indeed.

RECOMMENDED PANS:
Standard, mini, holes, twist

FOR THE DOUGHNUTS:
½ cup (60 g) oat flour
½ cup (70 g) sweet rice flour
⅓ cup (67 g) pure cane sugar
¼ cup (28 g) almond meal
I teaspoon baking powder
½ teaspoon salt
2 large eggs
¼ cup + 2 tablespoons (88 ml) milk
3 tablespoons (45 g) unsweetened
   applesauce
2 tablespoons (28 ml) oil
1½ teaspoons lemon zest
1½ teaspoons vanilla extract
⅓ cup (77 g) cream cheese,
   softened
½ cup (85 g) chopped
   strawberries

FOR THE FROSTING:
½ cup (115 g) cream cheese, softened
2½ tablespoons (35 g) butter, softened
I cup (120 g) powdered sugar
I teaspoon lemon zest
½ teaspoon vanilla extract

FOR THE TOPPING:
Chopped strawberries
Crushed gluten-free graham crackers

TO MAKE THE DOUGHNUTS: Preheat your oven to 350°F (180°C, or gas mark 4) and grease your doughnut pan.

Combine the oat flour, sweet rice flour, cane sugar, almond meal, baking powder, and salt in a large bowl, mixing well. In another bowl, whisk the eggs together. Then add in the milk, applesauce, oil, lemon zest, and vanilla extract. Whisk until well combined. Vigorously whisk in the cream cheese until it's broken apart and evenly distributed. The mixture will not be fully smooth.

Pour the wet mixture into the dry ingredients and stir with a large wooden spoon until just combined, being careful not to overmix (stop when you no longer see dry flour). Lightly blot the chopped strawberries with a paper towel and gently fold them into the batter.

Spoon the batter into the doughnut molds, filling to just below the top of each mold, ⅛- to ¼-inch (3 to 6 mm) from the top. Bake for 20 to 24 minutes until lightly golden brown around the edges. A toothpick inserted in the center should come out clean. Let cool in the pan for 5 minutes. Slide a thin spatula around the edges of the doughnuts to help loosen them out. Then place on a cooling rack and allow to cool fully before frosting.

TO MAKE THE FROSTING: Beat the cream cheese and butter together in a bowl until fluffy and smooth. Slowly beat in the powdered sugar until creamy and then beat in the lemon zest and vanilla extract.

Frost the doughnuts and then top with chopped strawberries (blot to dry if needed) and crushed graham crackers. These are best if served immediately after topping.

BANANA BREAD DOUGHNUTS
WITH CINNAMON GLAZE AND CRUNCHY WALNUTS

● ● ● ● ● ● ● ● ● ● ● ● ● ● ● ● *yield: 10 to 12 standard doughnuts* ● ● ● ● ● ● ● ● ● ● ● ● ● ● ●

While tasting just like your favorite banana bread, this doughnut is fluffier and more cake-like. I know there is a lot of debate about nuts or no nuts and if nuts, which nuts. I decided walnuts were the best fit for this creation, but feel free to change them up if you like or simply leave them out!

RECOMMENDED PANS:
Standard, mini, holes, twist

FOR THE DOUGHNUTS:
½ cup (60 g) oat flour
½ cup (70 g) sweet rice flour
¼ cup (28 g) almond meal
¼ cup (50 g) pure cane sugar
I teaspoon cinnamon
I teaspoon baking powder
½ teaspoon salt
2 large eggs
½ cup (113 g) mashed banana
¼ cup + 2 tablespoons (88 ml) milk
2 tablespoons (30 g) unsweetened
   applesauce
2 tablespoons (28 ml) oil
2 teaspoons vanilla extract
⅓ cup (40 g) chopped walnuts

FOR THE GLAZE:
I cup (120 g) powdered sugar
2 to 4 tablespoons (28 to 60 ml) milk
½ teaspoon vanilla extract
¼ teaspoon cinnamon

FOR THE TOPPING:
Chopped walnuts

TO MAKE THE DOUGHNUTS: Preheat your oven to 350°F (180°C, or gas mark 4) and grease your doughnut pan.

Combine the oat flour, sweet rice flour, almond meal, cane sugar, cinnamon, baking powder, and salt in a large bowl, mixing well. In another bowl, whisk the eggs together. Then add in the mashed banana, milk, applesauce, oil, and vanilla extract. Whisk until well combined.

Pour the wet mixture into the dry ingredients and stir with a large wooden spoon until just combined, being careful not to overmix (stop when you no longer see dry flour). Gently fold in the walnuts.

Spoon the batter into the doughnut molds, filling to just below the top of each mold, ⅛- to ¼-inch (3 to 6 mm) from the top. Bake for 18 to 22 minutes until lightly golden brown around the edges. A toothpick inserted in the center should come out clean. Let cool in the pan for 5 minutes. Slide a thin spatula around the edges of the doughnuts to help loosen them out. Then place on a cooling rack and allow to cool fully before topping.

TO MAKE THE GLAZE: Mix the glaze ingredients together until smooth. Add more milk if a thinner consistency is desired.

Invert the doughnut into the glaze, letting the excess drip off, or drizzle the glaze over the doughnut. Top with chopped walnuts. Let set until the glaze has hardened.

LEMON CAKE DOUGHNUTS
WITH LEMON VANILLA GLAZE

yield: 6 to 8 standard doughnuts

This recipe is all thanks to my mom. She makes a lemony bundt cake at least once a year that the entire family obsesses over. We all secretly hope for it on our birthday. I tried to transform that cake into doughnut form with this recipe. I even kept the traditional lemon-lime soda as the leavening agent. If you like lemon, you are going to love these.

RECOMMENDED PANS:
Standard, mini, holes, twist

FOR THE DOUGHNUTS:
½ cup (60 g) oat flour
½ cup (70 g) sweet rice flour
⅓ cup (67 g) pure cane sugar
3 tablespoons (21 g) almond meal
½ teaspoon salt
2 large eggs
⅓ cup (80 ml) lemon-lime soda
¼ cup (60 g) unsweetened applesauce
3 tablespoons (45 ml) oil
2 teaspoons lemon extract
1½ teaspoons lemon zest
1 teaspoon vanilla extract

FOR THE GLAZE:
1 cup (120 g) powdered sugar
2 to 3 tablespoons (28 to 45 ml) milk
1 teaspoon vanilla bean paste
½ teaspoon lemon extract

TO MAKE THE DOUGHNUTS: Preheat your oven to 350°F (180°C, or gas mark 4) and grease your doughnut pan.

Combine the oat flour, sweet rice flour, cane sugar, almond meal, and salt in a large bowl, mixing well. In another bowl, whisk the eggs together. Then add in the lemon-lime soda, applesauce, oil, lemon extract, lemon zest, and vanilla extract. Whisk until well combined.

Pour the wet mixture into the dry ingredients and stir with a large wooden spoon until just combined, being careful not to overmix (stop when you no longer see dry flour).

Spoon the batter into the doughnut molds filling to just below the top of each mold, ⅛- to ¼-inch (3 to 6 mm) from the top. Bake for 18 to 22 minutes until lightly golden brown around the edges. A toothpick inserted in the center should come out clean. Let cool in the pan for 5 minutes. Slide a thin spatula around the edges of the doughnuts to help loosen them out. Then place on a cooling rack and allow to cool fully before topping.

TO MAKE THE GLAZE: Mix the glaze ingredients together until smooth. Add more milk if a thinner consistency is desired.

Invert the doughnut into the glaze, letting the excess drip off, or drizzle the glaze over the doughnut. Let set until the glaze has hardened.

PEACH-STUFFED DOUGHNUTS
WITH VANILLA BEAN GLAZE

● ● ● ● ● ● ● ● ● ● ● ● ● ● ● *yield: 8 to 10 standard doughnuts* ● ● ● ● ● ● ● ● ● ● ● ● ● ●

Stuffed with plump peaches and topped with a vanilla bean glaze, this sweet, fruity treat is delightful. And I have to let you in on a little secret. Colorado has the best peaches you will ever try. However, no matter where your peaches come from, you will find these doughnuts irresistible.

RECOMMENDED PANS:
Standard

FOR THE DOUGHNUTS:
½ cup (60 g) oat flour
½ cup (70 g) sweet rice flour
⅓ cup (67 g) pure cane sugar
¼ cup (28 g) almond meal
I teaspoon baking powder
½ teaspoon salt
2 large eggs
¼ cup + 2 tablespoons (88 ml) unsweetened almond milk
3 tablespoons (45 g) unsweetened applesauce
2 tablespoons (28 ml) oil
2 teaspoons vanilla bean paste
½ cup (85 g) diced ripe peaches

FOR THE GLAZE:
I cup (120 g) powdered sugar
2 tablespoons (28 ml) milk
I teaspoon vanilla bean paste

FOR THE TOPPING:
I peach, thinly sliced from stem to end

TO MAKE THE DOUGHNUTS: Preheat your oven to 350°F (180°C, or gas mark 4) and grease your doughnut pan.

Combine the oat flour, sweet rice flour, cane sugar, almond meal, baking powder, and salt in a large bowl, mixing well. In another bowl, whisk the eggs together. Then add in the milk, applesauce, oil, and vanilla bean paste. Whisk until well combined.

Pour the wet mixture into the dry ingredients and stir with a large wooden spoon until just combined, being careful not to overmix (stop when you no longer see dry flour). Gently fold the peaches into the batter.

Spoon the batter into the doughnut molds, filling to just below the top of each mold, ⅛- to ¼-inch (3 to 6 mm) from the top. Bake for 20 to 24 minutes until lightly golden brown around the edges. A toothpick inserted in the center should come out clean. Let cool in the pan for 5 minutes. Slide a thin spatula around the edges of the doughnuts to help loosen them out. Then place on a cooling rack and allow to cool fully before topping.

TO MAKE THE GLAZE: Mix the ingredients together until smooth. Add more milk if a thinner consistency is desired.

Invert the doughnut into the glaze, letting the excess drip off, or drizzle the glaze over the doughnut. Let set until the glaze has hardened.

FOR THE TOPPING: Curl the thinly sliced peach and place in the center hole of the doughnut. Serve immediately.

fragrant &
spiced delights

WARM WAYS TO SCENT YOUR HOUSE
AND FILL YOUR BELLY.

· ·

The doughnuts in this chapter will lure you into the kitchen as the fragrance and spice emanate throughout your entire house. You will stand in front of the oven watching the minutes tick by until these fluffy, spiced creations are fully baked. Then get ready to top them with even more flavor and eat them by the baker's dozen.

· ·

PUMPKIN SPICE DOUGHNUTS
WITH MAPLE CINNAMON GLAZE

yield: 8 to 10 standard doughnuts

I love pumpkin. But I love the spices associated with pumpkin even more. This doughnut is filled to the brim with flavor and spice and is then topped with a maple-sweetened cinnamon glaze. Without a doubt an all-time favorite.

RECOMMENDED PANS:
Standard, mini, holes, twist

FOR THE DOUGHNUTS:
½ cup (60 g) oat flour
½ cup (70 g) sweet rice flour
¼ cup + 2 tablespoons (76 g) pure cane sugar
¼ cup (28 g) almond meal
1½ teaspoons cinnamon
1 teaspoon baking powder
½ teaspoon ginger
½ teaspoon nutmeg
½ teaspoon salt
¼ teaspoon allspice
⅛ teaspoon ground cloves
2 large eggs
¼ cup + 2 tablespoons (88 ml) milk
⅓ cup (82 g) pumpkin purée
2 tablespoons (30 g) unsweetened applesauce
2 tablespoons (28 ml) oil
1½ teaspoons vanilla extract

FOR THE GLAZE:
1 cup (120 g) powdered sugar
2 tablespoons (40 g) pure maple syrup
½ to 1 tablespoon (8 to 15 ml) milk
½ teaspoon cinnamon

TO MAKE THE DOUGHNUTS: Preheat your oven to 350°F (180°C, or gas mark 4) and grease your doughnut pan.

Combine the oat flour, sweet rice flour, cane sugar, almond meal, cinnamon, baking powder, ginger, nutmeg, salt, allspice, and ground cloves in a large bowl, mixing well. In another bowl, whisk the eggs together. Then add in the milk, pumpkin purée, applesauce, oil, and vanilla extract. Whisk until well combined.

Pour the wet mixture into the dry ingredients and stir with a large wooden spoon until just combined, being careful not to overmix (stop when you no longer see dry flour).

Spoon the batter into the doughnut molds filling to just below the top of each mold, ⅛- to ¼-inch (3 to 6 mm) from the top. Bake for 18 to 22 minutes, until lightly golden brown around the edges. A toothpick inserted in the center should come out clean. Let cool in the pan for 5 minutes. Slide a thin spatula around the edges of the doughnuts to help loosen them out. Then place on a cooling rack and allow to cool fully before topping.

TO MAKE THE GLAZE: Mix the glaze ingredients together until smooth. Add more milk if a thinner consistency is desired.

Invert the doughnut into the glaze, letting the excess drip off, or drizzle the glaze over the doughnut. Let set until the glaze has hardened.

RECIPE NOTE

Feel free to use 2 to 2½ teaspoons (4 to 5 g) of pumpkin pie spice instead of the cinnamon, ginger, nutmeg, allspice, and clove.

RUM RAISIN DOUGHNUTS
WITH BOOZY CREAM CHEESE FROSTING

yield: 8 to 10 standard doughnuts

A boozy doughnut? Why yes. Yes indeed. This lightly spiced cake is studded with rum-soaked raisins and topped with a honey-sweetened cream cheese frosting. The frosting is also infused with rum for a little extra kick.

RECOMMENDED PANS:
Standard, mini, holes, twist

FOR THE RUM RAISINS:
½ cup (75 g) raisins
¼ cup (60 ml) dark rum

FOR THE DOUGHNUTS:
½ cup (60 g) oat flour
½ cup (70 g) sweet rice flour
⅓ cup (67 g) pure cane sugar
3 tablespoons (21 g) almond meal
I teaspoon baking powder
½ teaspoon cinnamon
½ teaspoon salt
⅛ teaspoon nutmeg
⅛ teaspoon allspice
2 large eggs
⅓ cup (80 ml) milk
¼ cup (60 g) applesauce
2 tablespoons (28 ml) oil
I½ tablespoons (23 ml) dark rum
I½ teaspoons vanilla extract

FOR THE FROSTING:
¾ cup (173 g) cream cheese, softened
¼ cup + 2 tablespoons (120 g) honey
2 teaspoons dark rum
½ teaspoon cinnamon
⅛ teaspoon nutmeg
¾ teaspoon vanilla extract

FOR THE TOPPING:
Raisins

TO MAKE THE RUM RAISINS: Place the raisins and ¼ cup (60 ml) dark rum in a small bowl. Let soak for I hour. Drain the rum.

TO MAKE THE DOUGHNUTS: Preheat your oven to 350°F (180°C, or gas mark 4) and grease your doughnut pan.

Combine the oat flour, sweet rice flour, cane sugar, almond meal, baking powder, cinnamon, salt, nutmeg, and allspice in a large bowl, mixing well. In another bowl, whisk the eggs together. Then add in the milk, applesauce, oil, dark rum, and vanilla extract. Whisk until well combined.

Pour the wet mixture into the dry ingredients and stir with a large wooden spoon until just combined, being careful not to overmix (stop when you no longer see dry flour).

Spoon the batter into the doughnut molds, filling to just below the top of each mold, ⅛- to ¼-inch (3 to 6 mm) from the top. Bake for 18 to 22 minutes until lightly golden brown around the edges. A toothpick inserted in the center should come out clean. Let cool in the pan for 5 minutes. Slide a thin spatula around the edges of the doughnuts to help loosen them out. Then place on a cooling rack and allow to cool fully before topping.

TO MAKE THE FROSTING: Beat the cream cheese and honey together until creamy. Beat in the remaining ingredients until smooth. Spread the frosting over the doughnuts and top with raisins if desired.

STRAWBERRY LAVENDER DOUGHNUTS
WITH SWEET CREAM CHEESE FROSTING

yield: 8 to 10 standard doughnuts

Lavender grows in abundance where I live. These enormous and lightly purple-colored plants take over sidewalks and garden beds, sending a light fragrance through the fresh summer air. Strawberries bring sweetness and balance to the lavender aroma and flavor, while the frosting adds a soft, creamy finish.

RECOMMENDED PANS:
Standard, mini, holes, twist

FOR THE PURÉE:
1½ cups (255 g) strawberries, hulled and chopped
1 tablespoon (20 g) honey
1 teaspoon tapioca starch

FOR THE DOUGHNUTS:
½ cup (60 g) oat flour
½ cup (70 g) sweet rice flour
¼ cup + 2 tablespoons (76 g) pure cane sugar
3 tablespoons (21 g) almond meal
2½ teaspoons (4 g) ground dried lavender buds
1 teaspoon baking powder
¼ teaspoon salt
2 large eggs
7 tablespoons (102 g) strawberry purée
¼ cup + 2 tablespoons (88 ml) milk
2 tablespoons (28 ml) oil
1½ teaspoons vanilla extract

FOR THE FROSTING:
¾ cup (173 g) cream cheese, softened
¼ cup (55 g) butter, softened
¼ cup (30 g) powdered sugar
2 tablespoons (40 g) honey

FOR THE TOPPING:
Fresh strawberries, thinly sliced

TO MAKE THE PURÉE: Place the strawberries, honey, and tapioca starch into a pot over medium heat. Stir until the mixture comes to a boil, and then reduce the heat to simmer uncovered for 8 to 10 minutes until thickened and the strawberries start to break apart. Empty the mixture into a blender and purée. Let cool fully.

TO MAKE THE DOUGHNUTS: Preheat your oven to 350°F (180°C, or gas mark 4) and grease your doughnut pan.

Combine the oat flour, sweet rice flour, cane sugar, almond meal, ground lavender, baking powder, and salt in a large bowl, mixing well. In another bowl, whisk the eggs. Then add in the strawberry purée, milk, oil, and vanilla extract. Whisk until well combined.

Pour the wet mixture into the dry ingredients and stir with a large wooden spoon until just combined, being careful not to overmix (stop when you no longer see dry flour).

Spoon the batter into the doughnut molds, filling to just below the top of each mold, ⅛- to ¼-inch (3 to 6 mm) from the top. Bake for 20 to 24 minutes until lightly golden brown around the edges. A toothpick inserted in the center should come out clean. Let cool in the pan for 5 minutes. Slide a thin spatula around the edges of the doughnuts to help loosen them out. Then place on a cooling rack and allow to cool fully before icing.

TO MAKE THE FROSTING: Beat the cream cheese and butter together until fluffy and smooth. Slowly beat in the powdered sugar and honey until fully combined and creamy. Spread on the doughnuts and then top with thinly sliced strawberries (blot lightly to dry if needed). Serve immediately.

GINGERBREAD DOUGHNUTS
WITH SPICED GINGERBREAD GLAZE

● ● ● ● ● ● ● ● ● ● ● ● ● ● *yield: 8 to 10 standard doughnuts* ● ● ● ● ● ● ● ● ● ● ● ● ●

I'm not really a fan of crunchy gingerbread cookies, but add all of that lovely flavor into a doughnut and I'm sold. Top them with a gingerbread glaze and it's all over. You will have to fight me if you want one.

RECOMMENDED PANS:
Standard, mini, holes, twist

FOR THE DOUGHNUTS:
½ cup (60 g) oat flour
½ cup (70 g) sweet rice flour
⅓ cup (67 g) pure cane sugar
3 tablespoons (21 g) almond meal
2 teaspoons ginger
1½ teaspoons cinnamon
1 teaspoon baking powder
½ teaspoon nutmeg
½ teaspoon ground cloves
½ teaspoon salt
¼ teaspoon black pepper
2 large eggs
⅓ cup (80 ml) milk
3 tablespoons (45 g) unsweetened
    applesauce
2 tablespoons (40 g) molasses
2 tablespoons (28 ml) oil
1½ teaspoons vanilla extract

FOR THE GLAZE:
1 cup (120 g) powdered sugar
2 to 3 tablespoons (15 to 28 ml) milk
¼ teaspoon cinnamon
¼ teaspoon ginger
1/16 teaspoon ground cloves

TO MAKE THE DOUGHNUTS: Preheat your oven to 350°F (180°C, or gas mark 4) and grease your doughnut pan.

Combine the oat flour, sweet rice flour, cane sugar, almond meal, ginger, cinnamon, baking powder, nutmeg, ground cloves, salt, and black pepper in a large bowl, mixing well. In another bowl, whisk the eggs together. Then add in the milk, applesauce, molasses, oil, and vanilla extract. Whisk until well combined.

Pour the wet mixture into the dry ingredients and stir with a large wooden spoon until just combined, being careful not to overmix (stop when you no longer see dry flour).

Spoon the batter into the doughnut molds, filling to just below the top of each mold, ⅛- to ¼-inch (3 to 6 mm) from the top. Bake for 18 to 22 minutes until lightly golden brown around the edges. A toothpick inserted in the center should come out clean. Let cool in the pan for 5 minutes. Slide a thin spatula around the edges of the doughnuts to help loosen them out. Then place on a cooling rack and allow to cool fully before topping.

TO MAKE THE GLAZE: Mix the glaze ingredients together until smooth. Add more milk if a thinner consistency is desired. Invert the doughnut into the glaze, letting the excess drip off, or drizzle the glaze over the doughnut. Let set until the glaze has hardened.

GREEN MATCHA DOUGHNUTS
WITH VANILLA HONEY CREAM GLAZE

yield: 8 to 10 standard doughnuts

Green matcha tea is a high-quality, shade-grown tea that is ground into a fine powder and brews with a very smooth and silky flavor. That lovely, mellow flavor translates spectacularly well into baked goods, tasting very similar to an actual green matcha tea latte. As an added bonus, it turns the doughnut green. Now, what could be better than eating a green doughnut?

RECOMMENDED PANS:
Standard, mini, holes, twist

FOR THE DOUGHNUTS:
½ cup (60 g) oat flour
½ cup (70 g) sweet rice flour
⅓ cup (67 g) pure cane sugar
3 tablespoons (21 g) almond meal
I tablespoon (6 g) green matcha powder, culinary quality
I teaspoon baking powder
½ teaspoon salt
2 large eggs
¼ cup + 2 tablespoons (88 ml) milk
¼ cup (60 g) unsweetened applesauce
2 tablespoons (28 ml) oil
1½ teaspoons vanilla extract

FOR THE GLAZE:
2 tablespoons (30 g) cream cheese, softened
2 tablespoons (28 g) butter, softened
3 to 4 tablespoons (45 to 60 ml) half-and-half
3 tablespoons (60 g) honey
I cup (120 g) powdered sugar
I teaspoon vanilla bean paste

TO MAKE THE DOUGHNUTS: Preheat your oven to 350°F (180°C, or gas mark 4) and grease your doughnut pan.

Combine the oat flour, sweet rice flour, cane sugar, almond meal, matcha powder, baking powder, and salt in a large bowl, mixing well. In another bowl, whisk the eggs together. Then whisk in the milk, applesauce, oil, and vanilla extract.

Pour the wet mixture into the dry ingredients and stir with a large wooden spoon until just combined, being careful not to overmix (stop when you no longer see dry flour).

Spoon the batter into the doughnut molds, filling to just below the top of each mold, ⅛- to ¼-inch (3 to 6 mm) from the top. Bake for 18 to 22 minutes until lightly golden brown around the edges. A toothpick inserted in the center should come out clean. Let cool in the pan for 5 minutes. Slide a thin spatula around the edges of the doughnuts to help loosen them out. Then place on a cooling rack and allow to cool fully before topping.

TO MAKE THE GLAZE: Mix the glaze ingredients together until smooth. Add more half-and-half if a thinner consistency is desired. Beat the glaze ingredients with a mixer if needed.

Invert the doughnut and dunk it into the glaze, letting the excess drip off, or drizzle over the doughnuts. Let rest until the glaze has hardened.

CHAI-SPICED DOUGHNUTS
WITH CINNAMON VANILLA CREAM GLAZE

yield: 8 to 10 standard doughnuts

Can you imagine *eating* a chai latte? All of that chai latte flavor and spice wrapped up in a doughnut and topped with a creamy, sweet glaze. If you're wondering how this tastes eaten alongside an actual chai latte, the answer is better than good. As in, I highly recommend it.

RECOMMENDED PANS:
Standard, mini, holes, twist

FOR THE DOUGHNUTS:
½ cup (60 g) oat flour
½ cup (70 g) sweet rice flour
⅓ cup (67 g) pure cane sugar
3 tablespoons (21 g) almond meal
1¼ teaspoons cinnamon
1 teaspoon baking powder
¾ teaspoon ginger
½ teaspoon cardamom
½ teaspoon salt
¼ teaspoon allspice
¼ teaspoon ground cloves
⅛ teaspoon black pepper
2 large eggs
½ cup (120 ml) chai tea, brewed
   with milk and cooled
¼ cup (60 g) unsweetened applesauce
2 tablespoons (28 ml) oil
1½ teaspoons vanilla extract

FOR THE GLAZE:
1 cup (120 g) powdered sugar
3 to 4 tablespoons (45 to 60 ml)
   half-and-half
1 teaspoon vanilla bean paste
½ teaspoon cinnamon

TO MAKE THE DOUGHNUTS: Preheat your oven to 350°F (180°C, or gas mark 4) and grease your doughnut pan.

Combine the oat flour, sweet rice flour, cane sugar, almond meal, cinnamon, baking powder, ginger, cardamom, salt, allspice, ground cloves, and black pepper in a large bowl, mixing well. In another bowl, whisk the eggs together. Then whisk in the chai tea, applesauce, oil, and vanilla extract.

Pour the wet mixture into the dry ingredients and stir with a large wooden spoon until just combined, being careful not to overmix (stop when you no longer see dry flour).

Spoon the batter into the doughnut molds filling to just below the top of each mold, $1/8$- to ¼-inch (3 to 6 mm) from the top. Bake for 18 to 22 minutes until lightly golden brown around the edges. A toothpick inserted in the center should come out clean. Let cool in the pan for 5 minutes. Slide a thin spatula around the edges of the doughnuts to help loosen them out. Then place on a cooling rack and allow to cool fully before topping.

TO MAKE THE GLAZE: Mix the glaze ingredients together until smooth. Add more half-and-half if a thinner consistency is desired. Invert the doughnut and dunk it into the glaze, letting the excess drip off, or drizzle over the doughnuts. Let set until the glaze has hardened.

CINNAMON COFFEE CAKE DOUGHNUTS
WITH STREUSEL TOPPING AND MAPLE CREAM CHEESE GLAZE

yield: 8 to 10 standard doughnuts

This is a cinnamon-loaded doughnut that will get you through a Monday. It will also get you through Tuesday–Friday. It's the most delicious coffee dipping treat!

RECOMMENDED PANS:
Standard, mini, holes, twist

FOR THE FILLING:
⅓ cup (75 g) packed brown sugar
½ teaspoon cinnamon

FOR THE STREUSEL:
¼ cup + 2 tablespoons (85 g) butter, softened
⅓ cup (107 g) pure maple syrup
1¼ cups (100 g) gluten-free rolled oats
1 tablespoon (8 g) oat flour
1 teaspoon cinnamon

FOR THE DOUGHNUTS:
½ cup (60 g) oat flour
½ cup (70 g) sweet rice flour
3 tablespoons (21 g) almond meal
2 tablespoons (26 g) pure cane sugar
1 teaspoon baking powder
¾ teaspoon cinnamon
½ teaspoon salt
2 large eggs
¼ cup + 2 tablespoons (88 ml) buttermilk
¼ cup (60 g) unsweetened applesauce
3 tablespoons (60 g) pure maple syrup
2 tablespoons (28 ml) oil
2 teaspoons vanilla extract

FOR THE GLAZE:
¼ cup (60 g) cream cheese, softened
3 tablespoons (60 g) pure maple syrup
1 teaspoon cinnamon
¾ teaspoon vanilla extract
2 tablespoons (28 ml) milk

TO MAKE THE FILLING: Mix the brown sugar and cinnamon together with a fork until combined. Set aside.

TO MAKE THE STREUSEL: Mash the butter and maple syrup together until combined. Add in the oats, oat flour, and cinnamon and mash until combined. Set aside.

TO MAKE THE DOUGHNUTS: Preheat your oven to 350°F (180°C, or gas mark 4) and grease your doughnut pan.

Combine the oat flour, sweet rice flour, almond meal, cane sugar, baking powder, cinnamon, and salt in a large bowl, mixing well. In another bowl, whisk the eggs together. Then whisk in the buttermilk, applesauce, maple syrup, oil, and vanilla extract.

Pour the wet mixture into the dry and stir with a large wooden spoon until just combined, being careful not to overmix (stop when you no longer see dry flour).

Spoon the batter into the doughnut molds, filling just halfway. Sprinkle the filling evenly over top and fill each mold with the remaining batter, ⅛- to ¼-inch (3 to 6 mm) from the top. Sprinkle about 2 tablespoons (15 g) of the streusel mixture over top of each doughnut.

Bake for 18 to 22 minutes until lightly golden brown around the edges. A toothpick inserted in the center should come out clean. Let cool in the pan for 5 minutes. Slide a thin spatula around the edges of the doughnuts to help loosen them out. Then place on a cooling rack and allow to cool fully before topping.

TO MAKE THE GLAZE: Mix the cream cheese and maple syrup together until smooth. Mix in the cinnamon, vanilla extract, and milk until fully combined and smooth. Drizzle over the doughnuts and serve.

CHOCOLATE CAYENNE DOUGHNUTS
WITH SWEET AND SPICY CHOCOLATE COATING

yield: 10 to 12 standard doughnuts

This doughnut is slightly deceiving. Upon first bite you think, "oooh, a cinnamon chocolate doughnut," but as you take that second bite something starts to happen. A little kick of heat travels down your throat that will warm you through and through.

RECOMMENDED PANS:
Standard, mini, holes, twist

FOR THE DOUGHNUTS:
½ cup (60 g) oat flour
½ cup (70 g) sweet rice flour
½ cup (100 g) pure cane sugar
¼ cup + 1 tablespoon (25 g) unsweetened cocoa powder
3 tablespoons (21 g) almond meal
1 teaspoon baking powder
1 teaspoon cayenne pepper
¾ teaspoon cinnamon
½ teaspoon salt
2 large eggs
½ cup (120 ml) milk
¼ cup (60 g) unsweetened applesauce
2 tablespoons (40 g) maple syrup
2 tablespoons (28 ml) oil
2 teaspoons vanilla extract

FOR THE TOPPING:
½ cup (100 g) pure cane sugar
1 tablespoon (5 g) unsweetened
   cocoa powder
⅛ teaspoon cinnamon
⅛ teaspoon cayenne pepper
¼ cup (55 g) butter, melted

TO MAKE THE DOUGHNUTS: Preheat your oven to 350°F (180°C, or gas mark 4) and grease your doughnut pan.

Combine the oat flour, sweet rice flour, cane sugar, cocoa powder, almond meal, baking powder, cayenne pepper, cinnamon, and salt in a large bowl, mixing well. In another bowl, whisk the eggs together. Then whisk in the milk, applesauce, maple syrup, oil, and vanilla extract.

Pour the wet mixture into the dry ingredients and stir with a large wooden spoon until just combined, being careful not to overmix (stop when you no longer see dry flour).

Spoon the batter into the doughnut molds, filling to just below the top of each mold, ⅛- to ¼-inch (3 to 6 mm) from the top. Bake for 18 to 22 minutes, until lightly golden brown around the edges. A toothpick inserted in the center should come out clean. Let cool in the pan for 5 minutes. Slide a thin spatula around the edges of the doughnuts to help loosen them out. Then place on a cooling rack and allow to cool fully before topping.

TO MAKE THE TOPPING: Mix the sugar, cocoa powder, cinnamon, and cayenne pepper together in a bowl. Brush melted butter on the tops of the doughnuts. Dip the top of the doughnut into the sugar mixture and serve.

CARROT CAKE DOUGHNUTS
WITH CINNAMON CREAM CHEESE FROSTING

yield: 8 to 10 standard doughnuts

Unlike the banana bread doughnuts, I decided to make this doughnut sans nuts—at least on the inside. This may be my favorite doughnut, and I didn't even know I liked carrot cake. Just promise me one thing? You won't put pineapple in these!

RECOMMENDED PANS:
Standard, mini, holes, twist

FOR THE DOUGHNUTS:
½ cup (60 g) oat flour
½ cup (70 g) sweet rice flour
⅓ cup (67 g) pure cane sugar
¼ cup (28 g) almond meal
I teaspoon baking powder
I teaspoon cinnamon
½ teaspoon ginger
¼ teaspoon nutmeg
⅛ teaspoon allspice
½ teaspoon salt
2 large eggs
⅓ cup (80 ml) milk
¼ cup (60 g) unsweetened applesauce
2 tablespoons (40 g) pure maple syrup
2 tablespoons (28 ml) oil
1½ teaspoons vanilla extract
¾ cup (83 g) finely grated carrots

FOR THE FROSTING:
½ cup (115 g) cream cheese, softened
3 tablespoons (42 g) butter, softened
I cup (120 g) powdered sugar
I teaspoon vanilla extract
½ teaspoon cinnamon

FOR THE TOPPING:
Toasted unsweetened flaked coconut
Chopped toasted pecans

TO MAKE THE DOUGHNUTS: Preheat your oven to 350°F (180°C, or gas mark 4) and grease your doughnut pan.

Combine the oat flour, sweet rice flour, cane sugar, almond meal, baking powder, cinnamon, ginger, nutmeg, allspice, and salt in a large bowl, mixing well. In another bowl, whisk the eggs together. Then whisk in the milk, applesauce, maple syrup, oil, and vanilla extract.

Pour the wet mixture into the dry ingredients and stir with a large wooden spoon until just combined, being careful not to overmix (stop when you no longer see dry flour). Gently fold in the finely grated carrots.

Spoon the batter into the doughnut molds, filling to just below the top of each mold, ⅛- to ¼-inch (3 to 6 mm) from the top. Bake for 20 to 24 minutes until lightly golden brown around the edges. A toothpick inserted in the center should come out clean. Let cool in the pan for 5 minutes. Slide a thin spatula around the edges of the doughnuts to help loosen them out. Then place on a cooling rack and allow to cool fully before topping.

TO MAKE THE FROSTING: Beat the cream cheese and butter together until fluffy and smooth. Slowly beat in the powdered sugar until creamy. Beat in the vanilla extract and cinnamon until combined. Spread over the doughnuts and top with toasted coconut and pecans.

EGGNOG SPICED DOUGHNUTS
WITH VANILLA EGGNOG GLAZE

yield: 8 to 10 standard doughnuts

You may only be familiar with eggnog in its classic drink form, but even better than that is this eggnog doughnut. It's filled with richness and spice, finished with a creamy, sweet eggnog glaze and topped with a sprinkle of freshly ground fragrant nutmeg.

RECOMMENDED PANS:
Standard, mini, holes, twist

FOR THE DOUGHNUTS:
½ cup (60 g) oat flour
½ cup (70 g) sweet rice flour
⅓ cup (67 g) pure cane sugar
3 tablespoons (21 g) almond meal
1 teaspoon baking powder
½ teaspoon ground nutmeg
½ teaspoon salt
2 large eggs
¼ cup + 3 tablespoons (105 ml) eggnog
¼ cup (60 g) unsweetened applesauce
2 tablespoons (28 ml) oil
2 teaspoons vanilla extract

FOR THE GLAZE:
1 cup (120 g) powdered sugar
4 to 6 tablespoons (60 to 90 ml) eggnog
1 teaspoon vanilla bean paste

FOR THE TOPPING:
Nutmeg, freshly ground

TO MAKE THE DOUGHNUTS: Preheat your oven to 350°F (180°C, or gas mark 4) and grease your doughnut pan.

Combine the oat flour, sweet rice flour, cane sugar, almond meal, baking powder, nutmeg, and salt in a large bowl, mixing well. In another bowl, whisk the eggs together. Then whisk in the eggnog, applesauce, oil, and vanilla extract.

Pour the wet mixture into the dry ingredients and stir with a large wooden spoon until just combined, being careful not to overmix (stop when you no longer see dry flour).

Spoon the batter into the doughnut molds, filling to just below the top of each mold, ⅛- to ¼-inch (3 to 6 mm) from the top. Bake for 18 to 22 minutes until lightly golden brown around the edges. A toothpick inserted in the center should come out clean. Let cool in the pan for 5 minutes. Slide a thin spatula around the edges of the doughnuts to help loosen them out. Then place on a cooling rack and allow to cool fully before topping.

TO MAKE THE GLAZE: Mix the glaze ingredients together until smooth. Add more eggnog for a thinner consistency. Invert the doughnuts into the glaze, letting the excess drip off, or drizzle the glaze over each doughnut. Top with a pinch of nutmeg. Let set until the glaze has hardened.

CHOCOLATE CHIP ZUCCHINI BREAD DOUGHNUTS
WITH LIGHT CREAM CHEESE GLAZE

yield: 10 to 12 standard doughnuts

Every summer growing up, my dad grew zucchini. Monstrous-sized zucchini. He would pile them up on our porch and my mom and I knew what to do. Zucchini bread. Just when we thought the baking had ceased, he would stack up a few more and we'd be at it again. But this time with chocolate chips.

RECOMMENDED PANS:
Standard, mini, holes, twist

FOR THE DOUGHNUTS:
½ cup (60 g) oat flour
½ cup (70 g) sweet rice flour
⅓ cup (67 g) pure cane sugar
¼ cup (28 g) almond meal
I teaspoon baking powder
I½ teaspoons (3.5 g) cinnamon
½ teaspoon salt
2 large eggs
⅓ cup (80 ml) milk
¼ cup (60 g) unsweetened applesauce
2 tablespoons (40 g) pure maple syrup
2 tablespoons (28 ml) oil
I½ teaspoons vanilla extract
¾ cup (90 g) unpeeled grated zucchini
⅓ cup (40 g) chopped walnuts
¼ cup (44 g) dark chocolate chips

FOR THE GLAZE:
½ cup (II5 g) cream cheese, softened
¼ cup + 2 tablespoons (45 g) powdered sugar
3 to 5 tablespoons (45 to 75 ml) milk
I teaspoon vanilla extract

FOR THE TOPPING:
Shaved dark chocolate

TO MAKE THE DOUGHNUTS: Preheat your oven to 350°F (I80°C, or gas mark 4) and grease your doughnut pan.

Combine the oat flour, sweet rice flour, cane sugar, almond meal, baking powder, cinnamon, and salt in a large bowl, mixing well. In another bowl, whisk the eggs together. Then whisk in the milk, applesauce, maple syrup, oil, and vanilla extract.

Pour the wet mixture into the dry ingredients and stir with a large wooden spoon until just combined, being careful not to overmix (stop when you no longer see dry flour). Blot the grated zucchini with a paper towel to soak up excess moisture. Gently fold in the zucchini, walnuts, and chocolate chips.

Spoon the batter into the doughnut molds, filling to just below the top of each mold, ⅛- to ¼-inch (3 to 6 mm) from the top. Bake for 20 to 24 minutes until lightly golden brown around the edges. A toothpick inserted in the center should come out clean. Let cool in the pan for 5 minutes. Slide a thin spatula around the edges of the doughnuts to help loosen them out. Then place on a cooling rack and allow to cool fully before topping.

TO MAKE THE GLAZE: Beat the cream cheese until fluffy and smooth. Slowly beat in the powdered sugar until creamy. Beat in the milk and vanilla extract until smooth. Spread over each doughnut. Glaze will not set. Top with shaved dark chocolate if desired.

SWEET AND SPICY CURRY DOUGHNUTS
WITH TAHINI MAPLE GLAZE

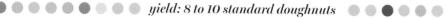

yield: 8 to 10 standard doughnuts

This curry doughnut actually takes a turn to the sweet side with the addition of pure cane sugar and honey. You'll feel a slight amount of heat with the addition of cayenne, but it will soon be calmed by the tahini maple glaze.

RECOMMENDED PANS:
Standard, mini, holes, twist

FOR THE DOUGHNUTS:
½ cup (60 g) oat flour
½ cup (70 g) sweet rice flour
¼ cup (50 g) pure cane sugar
3 tablespoons (21 g) almond meal
2 teaspoons curry powder
1 teaspoon baking powder
½ teaspoon cinnamon
½ teaspoon salt
¼ teaspoon cayenne pepper
⅛ teaspoon turmeric
2 large eggs
¼ cup + 2 tablespoons (88 ml) milk
¼ cup (60 g) unsweetened applesauce
3 tablespoons (60 g) honey
2 tablespoons (28 ml) oil
1 teaspoon vanilla extract

FOR THE GLAZE:
1 cup (120 g) powdered sugar
2 tablespoons (30 g) unsalted tahini
2 to 3 tablespoons (28 to 45 ml) milk
2 tablespoons (40 g) pure maple syrup
⅛ teaspoon cinnamon

TO MAKE THE DOUGHNUTS: Preheat your oven to 350°F (180°C, or gas mark 4) and grease your doughnut pan.

Combine the oat flour, sweet rice flour, cane sugar, almond meal, curry powder, baking powder, cinnamon, salt, cayenne pepper, and turmeric in a large bowl, mixing well. In another bowl, whisk the eggs together. Then whisk in the milk, applesauce, honey, oil, and vanilla extract.

Pour the wet mixture into the dry ingredients and stir with a large wooden spoon until just combined, being careful not to overmix (stop when you no longer see dry flour).

Spoon the batter into the doughnut molds, filling to just below the top of each mold, ⅛- to ¼-inch (3 to 6 mm) from the top. Bake for 18 to 22 minutes until lightly golden brown around the edges. A toothpick inserted in the center should come out clean. Let cool in the pan for 5 minutes. Slide a thin spatula around the edges of the doughnuts to help loosen them out. Then place on a cooling rack and allow to cool fully before topping.

TO MAKE THE GLAZE: Mix the glaze ingredients together until smooth. Add more milk if a thinner consistency is desired.

Invert the doughnut and dunk it into the glaze, letting the excess drip off, or drizzle over the doughnuts. Let set until the glaze has hardened.

MOLASSES DOUGHNUTS
WITH CRUNCHY SUGAR TOPPING

yield: 8 to 10 standard doughnuts

Every December my dad, brother, and I would make dozens of molasses cookies. I distinctly remember eating quite a bit of dough while rolling them into balls and dipping them in sugar. I also remember eating brown sugar straight from the bag. As a throwback to that childhood memory, I used the doughnut hole pan and dipped the doughnuts in sugar after baking. They look just like the raw cookie dough balls dipped in sugar right before we baked them—and taste even better.

RECOMMENDED PANS:
Standard, mini, holes, twist

FOR THE DOUGHNUTS:
½ cup (60 g) oat flour
½ cup (70 g) sweet rice flour
¼ cup (50 g) pure cane sugar
3 tablespoons (21 g) almond meal
1¼ teaspoons cinnamon
1 teaspoon baking powder
¾ teaspoon ginger
½ teaspoon salt
½ teaspoon ground ground cloves
2 large eggs
⅓ cup (80 ml) milk
3 tablespoons (60 g) molasses
3 tablespoons (45 g) unsweetened
    applesauce
2 tablespoons (28 ml) oil
1½ teaspoons vanilla extract

FOR THE TOPPING:
½ cup (50 g) pure cane sugar
3 tablespoons (42 g) butter, melted
¼ teaspoon cinnamon

TO MAKE THE DOUGHNUTS: Preheat your oven to 350°F (180°C, or gas mark 4) and grease your doughnut pan.

Combine the oat flour, sweet rice flour, cane sugar, almond meal, cinnamon, baking powder, ginger, salt, and ground cloves in a large bowl, mixing well. In another bowl, whisk the eggs together. Then wisk in the milk, molasses, applesauce, oil, and vanilla extract.

Pour the wet mixture into the dry ingredients and stir with a large wooden spoon until just combined, being careful not to overmix (stop when you no longer see dry flour).

Spoon the batter into the doughnut molds filling to just below the top of each mold, $\frac{1}{8}$- to ¼-inch (3 to 6 mm) from the top. Bake for 18 to 22 minutes until lightly golden brown around the edges. A toothpick inserted in the center should come out clean. Let cool in the pan for 5 minutes. Slide a thin spatula around the edges of the doughnuts to help loosen them out. Then place on a cooling rack and allow to cool fully before topping.

TO MAKE THE TOPPING: Mix the cinnamon and sugar together in a small bowl. Brush the tops of the doughnuts with the melted butter. Dip the tops of the doughnuts into the cinnamon-sugar mixture or dip both sides, if desired.

LEMON POPPY SEED DOUGHNUTS
WITH SWEET, LEMONY GLAZE

yield: 8 to 10 standard doughnuts

When I was asked what doughnuts were must-haves in this book, lemon poppy seed was named time and time again. This doughnut is bursting with lemony goodness and a lovely little crunch from the tiny poppy seeds. A classic muffin, turned doughnut, turned completely delicious—It won't disappoint!

RECOMMENDED PANS:
Standard, mini, holes, twist

FOR THE DOUGHNUTS:
½ cup (60 g) oat flour
½ cup (70 g) sweet rice flour
⅓ cup (67 g) pure cane sugar
3 tablespoons (21 g) almond meal
2½ tablespoons (23 g) poppy seeds
I teaspoon baking powder
½ teaspoon salt
2 large eggs
⅓ cup (80 ml) milk
¼ cup (60 g) unsweetened applesauce
2 tablespoons (28 ml) oil
I teaspoon vanilla extract
2 tablespoons (28 ml) lemon juice
I tablespoon + I teaspoon (8 g)
   lemon zest

FOR THE GLAZE:
I cup (120 g) powdered sugar
2 to 3 tablespoons (30 to 45 ml) lemon
   juice

FOR THE TOPPING:
Lemon zest

TO MAKE THE DOUGHNUTS: Preheat your oven to 350°F (180°C, or gas mark 4) and grease your doughnut pan.

Combine the oat flour, sweet rice flour, cane sugar, almond meal, poppy seeds, baking powder, and salt in a bowl, mixing well. In another bowl, whisk the eggs together. Then whisk in the milk, applesauce, oil, and vanilla extract. In a small bowl, whisk the lemon juice and zest together. Whisk into the wet mixture.

Pour the wet mixture into the dry ingredients and stir with a large wooden spoon until just combined, being careful not to overmix (stop when you no longer see dry flour).

Spoon the batter into the doughnut molds, filling to just below the top of each mold, ⅛- to ¼-inch (3 to 6 mm) from the top. Bake for 18 to 22 minutes until lightly golden brown around the edges. A toothpick inserted in the center should come out clean. Let cool in the pan for 5 minutes. Slide a thin spatula around the edges of the doughnuts to help loosen them out. Then place on a cooling rack and allow to cool fully before topping.

TO MAKE THE GLAZE: Mix the ingredients together until smooth. Add more lemon juice for a thinner consistency.

Invert doughnuts into the coating, letting the excess drip off, or drizzle over the doughnuts. Top with lemon zest and let set until the glaze has hardened.

CHAPTER 5

classic combinations

FOR THE KID IN US ALL.

· ·

I couldn't write a dessert cookbook without a chapter filled with classic combinations from sweets and treats I used to enjoy as a kid and a few grown-up flavors thrown in the mix as well. If you're thinking cookies and cream, orange cream soda, Almond Joy, and café mocha, you are on the right track.

· ·

PINEAPPLE RIGHT-SIDE-UP DOUGHNUTS
WITH SWEET GLAZE AND PINEAPPLE TOPPING

yield: 8 to 10 standard doughnuts

It's not upside down but right side up. These doughnuts are filled with crushed pineapple, turned right side up, and topped with a sweet glaze and chopped pineapple. They're pineapple lover's dream.

RECOMMENDED PANS:
Standard, holes, twist

FOR THE DOUGHNUTS:
½ cup (60 g) oat flour
½ cup (70 g) sweet rice flour
3 tablespoons (21 g) almond meal
⅓ cup (67 g) pure cane sugar
1 teaspoon baking powder
½ teaspoon salt
2 large eggs
6 tablespoons (90 ml) full-fat
   canned coconut milk, whisked
¼ cup (60 g) unsweetened applesauce
2 tablespoons (28 ml) oil
1½ teaspoons vanilla extract
¼ cup (48 g) crushed fresh pineapple

FOR THE GLAZE:
1 cup (125 g) pure cane sugar
¼ cup (55 g) butter, melted

FOR THE TOPPING:
Chopped pineapple

TO MAKE THE DOUGHNUTS: Preheat your oven to 350°F (180°C, or gas mark 4) and grease your doughnut pan.

Combine the oat flour, sweet rice flour, almond meal, cane sugar, baking powder, and salt in a large bowl, mixing well. In another bowl, whisk the eggs together. Then whisk in the coconut milk, applesauce, oil, and vanilla extract.

Pour the wet mixture into the dry ingredients and stir with a large wooden spoon until just combined, being careful not to overmix (stop when you no longer see dry flour). Gently fold in the pineapple.

Spoon the batter into the doughnut molds, filling to just below the top of each mold, ⅛- to ¼-inch (3 to 6 mm) from the top. Bake for 20 to 24 minutes until lightly golden brown around the edges. A toothpick inserted in the center should come out clean. Let cool in the pan for 5 minutes. Slide a thin spatula around the edges of the doughnuts to help loosen them out. Then place on a cooling rack and allow to cool fully before topping.

TO MAKE THE GLAZE: Stir the ingredients together until combined and brush or spoon over the doughnuts. The glaze will not be smooth. Top with chopped pineapple and serve.

ALMOND JOY DOUGHNUTS
WITH ALMONDS AND CHOCOLATE COATING

yield: 10 to 12 standard doughnuts

After taking the first bite of this doughnut, I was overjoyed (no pun intended). It is absolutely packed with coconut, just like the famous coconutty candy. To make it look and taste even more familiar, it's topped with a few raw almonds and smothered in a melted chocolate coating.

RECOMMENDED PANS:
Standard, twist

FOR THE DOUGHNUTS:
1 cup (80 g) unsweetened shredded
    coconut
½ cup (60 g) oat flour
½ cup (70 g) sweet rice flour
⅓ cup (67 g) pure cane sugar
3 tablespoons (21 g) almond meal
1 teaspoon baking powder
½ teaspoon salt
2 large eggs
½ cup + 2 tablespoons (148 ml) lite
    canned coconut milk
¼ cup (60 g) unsweetened applesauce
2 tablespoons (28 ml) oil
1½ teaspoons vanilla extract

FOR THE COATING:
1½ cups (263 g) dark chocolate chips
1½ tablespoons (21 g) coconut oil

FOR THE TOPPING:
Whole roasted almonds, unsalted

TO MAKE THE DOUGHNUTS: Preheat your oven to 350°F (180°C, or gas mark 4) and grease your doughnut pan.

Combine the coconut, oat flour, sweet rice flour, cane sugar, almond meal, baking powder, and salt in a large bowl, mixing well. In another bowl, whisk the eggs together. Then whisk in the coconut milk, applesauce, oil, and vanilla extract.

Pour the wet mixture into the dry ingredients and stir with a large wooden spoon until just combined, being careful not to overmix (stop when you no longer see dry flour).

Spoon the batter into the doughnut molds, filling to just below the top of each mold, ⅛- to ¼-inch (3 to 6 mm) from the top. Bake for 18 to 22 minutes until lightly golden brown around the edges. A toothpick inserted in the center should come out clean. Let cool in the pan for 5 minutes. Slide a thin spatula around the edges of the doughnuts to help loosen them out. Then place on a cooling rack and allow to cool fully before topping.

TO MAKE THE COATING: Melt the chocolate and coconut oil in a double boiler, stirring until smooth, or place in a small microwave-safe bowl and microwave for 30-second increments, stirring after each interval, until smooth.

Turn the doughnuts smooth side up and place on a wire rack. Dab four almonds into the chocolate and place around the doughnut. Using a spoon, slowly pour the chocolate over the almonds and doughnuts until the tops and sides are fully covered. Let set until the chocolate has hardened.

ORANGE CREAM SODA DOUGHNUTS
WITH ORANGE CREAM GLAZE

● ● ● ● ● ● ● ● ● ● ● ● ● ● ● ● *yield: 8 to 10 standard doughnuts* ● ● ● ● ● ● ● ● ● ● ● ● ● ● ● ●

These doughnuts taste creamy and are bursting with a bright orange flavored POP, just like the soda. The creamy vanilla glaze is the icing on the cake—or doughnut.

RECOMMENDED PANS:
Standard, mini, holes, twist

FOR THE DOUGHNUTS:
½ cup (60 g) oat flour
½ cup (70 g) sweet rice flour
⅓ cup (67 g) pure cane sugar
3 tablespoons (21 g) almond meal
¾ teaspoon baking powder
½ teaspoon salt
2 large eggs
⅓ cup (80 ml) orange cream soda
¼ cup (60 g) unsweetened applesauce
2 tablespoons (28 ml) oil
2 teaspoons orange zest
I teaspoon vanilla extract

FOR THE GLAZE:
2 tablespoons (30 g) cream cheese, softened
I cup (120 g) powdered sugar
2 to 3 tablespoons (28 to 45 ml) half-and-half
I teaspoon vanilla bean paste
I teaspoon orange zest

TO MAKE THE DOUGHNUTS: Preheat your oven to 350°F (180°C, or gas mark 4) and grease your doughnut pan.

Combine the oat flour, sweet rice flour, cane sugar, almond meal, baking powder, and salt in a large bowl, mixing well. In another bowl, whisk the eggs together. Then whisk in the orange cream soda, applesauce, oil, orange zest, and vanilla extract.

Pour the wet mixture into the dry ingredients and stir with a large wooden spoon until just combined, being careful not to overmix (stop when you no longer see dry flour).

Spoon the batter into the doughnut molds, filling to just below the top of each mold, ⅛- to ¼-inch (3 to 6 mm) from the top. Bake for 18 to 22 minutes until lightly golden brown around the edges. A toothpick inserted in the center should come out clean. Let cool in the pan for 5 minutes. Slide a thin spatula around the edges of the doughnuts to help loosen them out. Then place on a cooling rack and allow to cool fully before topping.

TO MAKE THE GLAZE: Mash the cream cheese and powdered sugar together until combined. Mix in the half-and-half starting with 2 tablespoons (28 ml), and the vanilla bean paste. Add more half-and-half if a thinner consistency is desired. The glaze should be creamy and smooth. Use a hand mixer if necessary. Stir in the orange zest. Invert the doughnut into the glaze, letting the excess drip off, or drizzle the glaze over the doughnut. Let the doughnuts set until the glaze has hardened.

CAFÉ MOCHA DOUGHNUTS
WITH CHOCOLATE ESPRESSO CREAM GLAZE

yield: 8 to 10 standard doughnuts

The first fancy coffee beverage I ever sipped on was a café mocha. It will always be a favorite, which is why this café mocha doughnut was a must. Not only is the doughnut filled with espresso and cocoa but so is the glaze. They're double trouble. This doughnut may leave you with a little coffee buzz.

RECOMMENDED PANS:
Standard, mini, holes, twist

FOR THE DOUGHNUTS:
½ cup (60 g) oat flour
½ cup (70 g) sweet rice flour
½ cup (100 g) pure cane sugar
¼ cup (20 g) unsweetened cocoa powder
3 tablespoons (21 g) almond meal
I tablespoon + I teaspoon (5 g) instant
   espresso powder
I teaspoon baking powder
½ teaspoon salt
2 large eggs
½ cup + 2 tablespoons (148 ml) milk
¼ cup (60 g) unsweetened applesauce
2 tablespoons (28 ml) oil
2 teaspoons vanilla extract

FOR THE GLAZE:
I cup (120 g) powdered sugar
1½ tablespoons (23 g) cream cheese,
   softened
1½ tablespoons (8 g) unsweetened
   cocoa powder
2 to 3 tablespoons (28 to 60 ml)
   half-and-half
I teaspoon vanilla extract
½ teaspoon espresso powder

FOR THE DRIZZLE:
¼ cup (30 g) powdered sugar
2 to 3 teaspoons (10 to 15 ml) half-
   and-half
¼ teaspoon vanilla extract

TO MAKE THE DOUGHNUTS: Preheat your oven to 350°F (180°C, or gas mark 4) and grease your doughnut pan.

Combine the oat flour, sweet rice flour, pure cane sugar, cocoa powder, almond meal, instant espresso powder, baking powder, and salt in a large bowl, mixing well. In another bowl, whisk the eggs together. Then whisk in the milk, applesauce, oil, and vanilla extract.

Pour the wet mixture into the dry ingredients and stir with a large wooden spoon until just combined, being careful not to overmix (stop when you no longer see dry flour).

Spoon the batter into the doughnut molds, filling to just below the top of each mold, $^1/_8$- to ¼-inch (3 to 6 mm) from the top. Bake for 18 to 22 minutes until lightly golden brown around the edges. A toothpick inserted in the center should come out clean. Let cool in the pan for 5 minutes. Slide a thin spatula around the edges of the doughnuts to help loosen them out. Then place on a cooling rack and allow to cool fully before topping.

TO MAKE THE GLAZE: Mash the powdered sugar and cream cheese together until combined. Mix in the rest of the glaze ingredients together until smooth. Add more half-and-half for a thinner consistency. Beat with a mixer if needed.

Invert the doughnut and dunk it into the glaze, letting the excess drip off, or drizzle over the doughnuts. Let set until the glaze has hardened and then add the drizzle.

TO MAKE THE DRIZZLE: Mix the drizzle ingredients together until smooth. Drizzle over the glaze and let set until the drizzle has hardened.

CAPPUCCINO DOUGHNUTS
WITH SWEET CREAM GLAZE

yield: 8 to 10 standard doughnuts

I have the hardest time deciding between ordering a cappuccino or a latte. Oftentimes, I forget the difference between the two. This doughnut solves that problem. Now I can order a latte and *eat* a cappuccino—a cappuccino doughnut that is filled with espresso and topped with a rich, creamy glaze.

RECOMMENDED PANS:
Standard, mini, holes, twist

FOR THE DOUGHNUTS:
½ cup (60 g) oat flour
½ cup (70 g) sweet rice flour
½ cup (100 g) pure cane sugar
3 tablespoons (21 g) almond meal
1½ tablespoons (6 g) instant espresso powder
1 teaspoon baking powder
½ teaspoon salt
2 large eggs
¼ cup + 2 tablespoons (88 ml) milk
¼ cup (60 g) unsweetened applesauce
2 tablespoons (28 ml) oil
2 teaspoons vanilla extract

FOR THE GLAZE:
1 cup (120 g) powdered sugar
½ tablespoon cream cheese, softened
2 to 3 tablespoons (28 to 45 ml) half-and-half

TO MAKE THE DOUGHNUTS: Preheat your oven to 350°F (180°C, or gas mark 4) and grease your doughnut pan.

Combine the oat flour, sweet rice flour, cane sugar, almond meal, instant espresso powder, baking powder, and salt in a large bowl, mixing well. In another bowl, whisk the eggs together. Then whisk in the milk, applesauce, oil, and vanilla extract.

Pour the wet mixture into the dry ingredients and stir with a large wooden spoon until just combined, being careful not to overmix (stop when you no longer see dry flour).

Spoon the batter into the doughnut molds filling to just below the top of each mold, ⅛- to ¼-inch (3 to 6 mm) from the top. Bake for 18 to 22 minutes until lightly golden brown around the edges. A toothpick inserted in the center should come out clean. Let cool in the pan for 5 minutes. Slide a thin spatula around the edges of the doughnuts to help loosen them out. Then place on a cooling rack and allow to cool fully before topping.

TO MAKE THE GLAZE: Mix the glaze ingredients together until smooth. Add more half-and-half for a thinner consistency. Beat with a mixer if needed.

Invert the doughnut and dunk it into the glaze, letting the excess drip off, or drizzle over the doughnuts. Let the doughnuts rest until the glaze has hardened.

ROCKY ROAD DOUGHNUTS
WITH CHOCOLATE, MARSHMALLOW, AND PEANUTS

yield: 12 to 14 standard doughnuts

When you feel the need for a slightly messy, super-chocolaty, marshmallow- and peanut-topped doughnut, this will fit the bill. It's stuffed, smeared, and drizzled with all your favorite Rocky Road toppings.

RECOMMENDED PANS:
Standard

FOR THE DOUGHNUTS:
½ cup (60 g) oat flour
½ cup (70 g) sweet rice flour
½ cup (100 g) pure cane sugar
¼ cup (20 g) unsweetened cocoa powder
3 tablespoons (21 g) almond meal
1 teaspoon baking powder
½ teaspoon salt
2 large eggs
½ cup + 2 tablespoons (148 ml) milk
¼ cup (60 g) unsweetened applesauce
2 tablespoons (28 ml) oil
2 teaspoons vanilla extract
⅓ cup (58 g) dark chocolate chips
⅓ cup (48 g) partially ground peanuts

FOR THE COATING:
¾ cup (131 g) dark chocolate chips
⅓ cup (17 g) chopped marshmallows
1 tablespoon (14 g) coconut oil

FOR THE DRIZZLE:
¼ cup (44 g) chocolate chips
1 teaspoon coconut oil

FOR THE TOPPING:
Marshmallows
Chopped peanuts

TO MAKE THE DOUGHNUTS: Preheat your oven to 350°F (180°C, or gas mark 4) and grease your doughnut pan.

Combine the oat flour, sweet rice flour, cane sugar, cocoa powder, almond meal, baking powder, and salt in a large bowl, mixing well. In another bowl, whisk the eggs together. Then add in the milk, applesauce, oil, and vanilla extract. Whisk until well combined.

Pour the wet mixture into the dry ingredients and stir with a large wooden spoon until just combined, being careful not to overmix (stop when you no longer see dry flour). Gently fold in the chocolate chips and peanuts.

Spoon the batter into the doughnut molds, filling to just below the top of each mold, ⅛- to ¼-inch (3 to 6 mm) from the top. Bake for 18 to 22 minutes until lightly golden brown around the edges. A toothpick inserted in the center should come out clean. Let cool in the pan for 5 minutes. Slide a thin spatula around the edges of the doughnuts to help loosen them out. Then place on a cooling rack and allow to cool fully before topping.

TO MAKE THE COATING: Place the coating ingredients in a saucepan and heat gently over medium-low heat, stirring constantly. Stir until the ingredients are combined and the marshmallows have melted into the chocolate. The mixture will be very thick and sticky and not completely smooth.

Scrape the mixture into a bowl and while hot, carefully invert the doughnut into the coating and then place on a cooling rack for 5 minutes. Top the center of the doughnut with marshmallows (chop them if needed) and chopped peanuts. Let cool.

TO MAKE THE DRIZZLE: Melt the chocolate and coconut oil in a double boiler, stirring until smooth, or place in a small microwave-safe bowl and microwave for 30-second increments, stirring after each interval, until smooth. Drizzle over the doughnuts and let set until the drizzle has hardened.

KEY LIME DOUGHNUTS
WITH AVOCADO-LIME GLAZE

yield: 6 to 8 standard doughnuts

This was actually one of the first doughnut recipes I created back in the summer of 2011. My parents are huge key lime pie fans, so when they were coming to town, I whipped up a batch of these. Who knew they would ever be in an actual cookbook?

RECOMMENDED PANS:
Standard, mini, holes, twist

FOR THE DOUGHNUTS:
½ cup (60 g) oat flour
½ cup (70 g) sweet rice flour
⅓ cup (67 g) pure cane sugar
3 tablespoons (21 g) coconut flour
1 tablespoon (7 g) almond meal
1 teaspoon baking powder
½ teaspoon salt
2 large eggs
½ cup (120 ml) milk
3 tablespoons (45 g) unsweetened
   applesauce
2 tablespoons (28 ml) oil
1½ tablespoons (23 ml) lime juice
1½ tablespoons (9 g) lime zest
1½ teaspoons vanilla extract

FOR THE AVOCADO-LIME GLAZE:
1 ripe avocado
½ to ¾ cup (60 to 90 g) powdered sugar
1½ tablespoons (23 ml) lime juice
1 tablespoon (6 g) lime zest
Crushed gluten-free graham crackers

FOR THE LIME GLAZE:
1 cup (120 g) powdered sugar
1 to 2 tablespoons (28 to 45 ml) milk
2 teaspoons lime juice
2 tablespoons (12 g) lime zest
Crushed gluten-free graham crackers
   to top

TO MAKE THE DOUGHNUTS: Preheat your oven to 350°F (180°C, or gas mark 4) and grease your doughnut pan.

Combine the oat flour, sweet rice flour, cane sugar, coconut flour, almond meal, baking powder, and salt in a large bowl, mixing well. In another bowl, whisk the eggs together. Then whisk in the milk, applesauce, oil, lime juice, lime zest, and vanilla extract.

Pour the wet mixture into the dry ingredients and stir with a large wooden spoon until just combined, being careful not to overmix (stop when you no longer see dry flour).

Spoon the batter into the doughnut molds, filling to just below the top of each mold, ⅛- to ¼-inch (3 to 6 mm) from the top. Bake for 18 to 22 minutes until lightly golden brown around the edges. A toothpick inserted in the center should come out clean. Let cool in the pan for 5 minutes. Slide a thin spatula around the edges of the doughnuts to help loosen them out. Then place on a cooling rack and allow to cool fully before topping.

TO MAKE THE AVOCADO-LIME GLAZE: Add the avocado, ½ cup (60 g) powdered sugar, and lime juice to a blender or food processor. Blend until smooth. Add more lime juice to thin out if desired. Mix in the lime zest. Spread the glaze on the doughnuts. This glaze will not harden. Top with crushed graham crackers and serve immediately.

TO MAKE THE LIME GLAZE: Mix ingredients together until smooth, adding more milk if a thinner consistency is desired. Invert the doughnut into the glaze, letting the excess drip off, or drizzle the glaze over the doughnut. Top with crushed graham crackers. Let set until the glaze has hardened.

S'MORES DOUGHNUTS
WITH S'MORES TOPPINGS

yield: 8 to 10 standard doughnuts

This s'mores doughnut was one of my first doughnut creations and is a crowd-pleaser for all ages. S'mores just never get old. That gooey marshmallow, that creamy, melted chocolate, that graham cracker crunch—and now it's all sitting on top of a chocolate-laced vanilla doughnut. Yum.

RECOMMENDED PANS:
Standard

FOR THE DOUGHNUTS:
½ cup (60 g) oat flour
½ cup (70 g) sweet rice flour
⅓ cup (67 g) pure cane sugar
⅓ cup (43 g) ground dark chocolate chips
3 tablespoons (21 g) almond meal
1 teaspoon baking powder
½ teaspoon salt
2 large eggs
¼ cup + 2 tablespoons (88 ml) milk
¼ cup (60 g) unsweetened applesauce
2 tablespoons (28 ml) oil
2 teaspoons vanilla extract

FOR THE TOPPING:
Marshmallows, halved
Gluten-free graham crackers, broken up

FOR THE DRIZZLE:
½ cup (88 g) chocolate chips
½ tablespoon coconut oil

TO MAKE THE DOUGHNUTS: Preheat your oven to 350°F (180°C, or gas mark 4) and grease your doughnut pan.

Combine the oat flour, sweet rice flour, cane sugar, ground chocolate, almond meal, baking powder, and salt in a bowl, mixing well. In another bowl, whisk the eggs together. Add in the milk, applesauce, oil, and vanilla extract. Whisk until well combined.

Pour the wet mixture into the dry ingredients and stir with a large wooden spoon until just combined, being careful not to overmix (stop when you no longer see dry flour). Spoon the batter into the doughnut molds, filling to just below the top of each mold, ⅛- to ¼-inch (3 to 6 mm) from the top. Bake for 18 to 22 minutes until lightly golden brown around the edges. A toothpick inserted in the center should come out clean. Let cool in the pan for 5 minutes. Slide a thin spatula around the edges of the doughnuts to help loosen them out. Then place on a cooling rack and allow to cool fully before topping.

TO MAKE THE TOPPING: Preheat your oven to broil over low heat and position a rack in the top slot. Place an oven-safe wire rack on a rimmed baking sheet.

Place 4 to 6 marshmallow halves sticky side down on top of each doughnut. (If using full-sized marshmallows, you may want to quarter them.) Place under the broiler with the door cracked open until the marshmallows are golden brown, about 1 to 3 minutes. Watch closely so they don't burn. Remove from the oven and let cool for 3 to 4 minutes.

TO MAKE THE DRIZZLE: Melt the chocolate and coconut oil in a double boiler, stirring until smooth, or place in a small microwave-safe bowl and microwave for 30-second increments, stirring after each interval, until smooth. Drizzle over the doughnuts, sprinkle with the broken graham crackers, and drizzle more chocolate over top. Serve warm.

MARBLE CAKE DOUGHNUTS
WITH CHOCOLATE VANILLA BEAN CREAM GLAZE

 *yield: 8 to 10 standard doughnuts*

Do you find yourself wavering between vanilla and chocolate? Do you love marble cake and chocolate vanilla swirl ice cream? Then this will be your go-to doughnut. It's layered with chocolate and vanilla and topped with a vanilla bean chocolate cream glaze. It's the perfect "I just can't make up my mind" doughnut!

RECOMMENDED PANS:
Standard, mini, holes, twist

FOR THE VANILLA DOUGHNUTS:
¼ cup (30 g) oat flour
¼ cup (35 g) sweet rice flour
1½ tablespoons (11 g) almond meal
2½ tablespoons (33 g) pure cane sugar
½ teaspoon baking powder
¼ teaspoon salt
1 large egg
3 tablespoons (45 ml) milk
2 tablespoons (30 g) unsweetened
    applesauce
1 tablespoon (15 ml) oil
1 teaspoon vanilla extract

FOR THE CHOCOLATE DOUGHNUTS:
¼ cup (30 g) oat flour
¼ cup (35 g) sweet rice flour
1½ tablespoons (11 g) almond meal
2½ tablespoons (13 g) unsweetened
    cocoa powder
¼ cup (50 g) pure cane sugar
½ teaspoon baking powder
¼ teaspoon salt
1 large egg
¼ cup + 1 tablespoon (75 ml) milk
2 tablespoons (30 g) unsweetened
    applesauce
1½ tablespoons (23 ml) oil
1 teaspoon vanilla extract

FOR THE GLAZE:
1 cup (120 g) powdered sugar
1 tablespoon (5 g) unsweetened cocoa powder
3 to 4 tablespoons (45 to 60 ml) half-and-half
1 vanilla bean, scraped

TO MAKE THE VANILLA DOUGHNUTS: Preheat your oven to 350°F (180°C, or gas mark 4) and grease your doughnut pan.

Combine the oat flour, sweet rice flour, almond meal, cane sugar, baking powder, and salt in a large bowl, mixing well. In another bowl, whisk the egg. Then whisk in the milk, applesauce, oil, and vanilla extract.

Pour the wet mixture into the dry ingredients and stir with a large wooden spoon until just combined, being careful not to overmix (stop when you no longer see dry flour).

TO MAKE THE CHOCOLATE DOUGHNUTS: Follow the instructions for vanilla doughnuts, except add cocoa powder along with the other dry ingredients. Follow the ingredient amounts per the chocolate doughnut ingredient list.

Spoon the batter alternating between the vanilla and chocolate batters (for the marbled look) into the doughnut molds, filling to just below the top of each mold, $1/8$- to ¼-inch (3 to 6 mm) from the top. Bake for 18 to 22 minutes until lightly golden brown around the edges. A toothpick inserted in the center should come out clean. Let cool in the pan for 5 minutes. Slide a thin spatula around the edges of the doughnuts to help loosen them out. Then place on a cooling rack and allow to cool fully before topping.

TO MAKE THE GLAZE: Mix the glaze ingredients together until smooth. Add more half-and-half for a thinner consistency. Invert the doughnut into the glaze, letting the excess drip off, or drizzle over the doughnuts. Let set until the glaze has hardened.

PEANUT BUTTER CUP DOUGHNUTS
WITH CHOCOLATE PEANUT BUTTER COATING

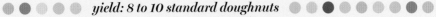

yield: 8 to 10 standard doughnuts

This doughnut was created for my husband, the ultimate peanut butter cup lover. I keep a stash of homemade peanut butter cups in our freezer at all times just for him. This doughnut is packed with peanut butter and coated in melted chocolate and even more peanut butter. Just as it should be.

RECOMMENDED PANS:
Standard, mini, holes, twist

FOR THE DOUGHNUTS:
½ cup (60 g) oat flour
½ cup (70 g) sweet rice flour
⅓ cup (67 g) pure cane sugar
3 tablespoons (27 g) peanut meal
I teaspoon baking powder
½ teaspoon salt
¼ teaspoon cinnamon
2 large eggs
½ cup (120 ml) milk
¼ cup (60 g) unsweetened applesauce
¼ cup (65 g) creamy peanut butter,
   melted and slightly cooled
I tablespoon (15 ml) oil
1½ teaspoons vanilla extract

FOR THE COATING:
I cup (175 g) dark chocolate chips
3 tablespoons (48 g) creamy peanut
   butter

FOR THE TOPPING:
Sprinkles
Large flaked sea salt

TO MAKE THE DOUGHNUTS: Preheat your oven to 350°F (180°C, or gas mark 4) and grease your doughnut pan.

Combine the oat flour, sweet rice flour, cane sugar, peanut meal, baking powder, salt, and cinnamon in a large bowl, mixing well. In another bowl, whisk the eggs together. Then whisk in the milk, applesauce, peanut butter, oil, and vanilla extract.

Pour the wet mixture into the dry ingredients and stir with a large wooden spoon until just combined, being careful not to overmix (stop when you no longer see dry flour).

Spoon the batter into the doughnut molds, filling to just below the top of each mold, ⅛- to ¼-inch (3 to 6 mm) from the top. Bake for 18 to 22 minutes until lightly golden brown around the edges. A toothpick inserted in the center should come out clean. Let cool in the pan for 5 minutes. Slide a thin spatula around the edges of the doughnuts to help loosen them out. Then place on a cooling rack and allow to cool fully before topping.

TO MAKE THE COATING: In a double boiler, stirring until smooth, melt the chocolate chips and peanut butter together, or place the chocolate in a small microwave-safe bowl and microwave for 30-second increments, stirring after each interval, until smooth. Stir in the peanut butter.

Invert the doughnut and dunk it into the coating, letting the excess drip off, or drizzle over the doughnuts. Top with sprinkles and a pinch of sea salt over each doughnut. Let set until the coating has hardened.

RECIPE NOTE

Peanut meal can be made at home by following the same instructions for making almond meal on page II. Use raw, unsalted, skinless peanuts.

COOKIES AND CREAM DOUGHNUTS
WITH BUTTER CREAM COOKIE FROSTING

yield: 8 to 10 standard doughnuts

The hot debate growing up was always cookies and cream ice cream or mint chocolate chip. I could never decide between the two, but this doughnut is a clear winner. Cookies and cream are packed inside the doughnut, inside the frosting, and then crushed over top to finish things off. The inner child in you is going to love this.

RECOMMENDED PANS:
Standard, mini, holes, twist

FOR THE DOUGHNUTS:
½ cup (60 g) oat flour
½ cup (70 g) sweet rice flour
⅓ cup (67 g) pure cane sugar
3 tablespoons (21 g) almond meal
I teaspoon baking powder
½ teaspoon salt
2 large eggs
¼ cup + 2 tablespoons (88 ml) milk
¼ cup (60 g) unsweetened applesauce
2 tablespoons (28 ml) oil
1½ teaspoons vanilla extract
½ cup (45 g) crushed gluten-free
  cookies and cream cookies

FOR THE FROSTING:
½ cup (112 g) butter
2 tablespoons (30 g) cream cheese
¾ to I cup (90 to 120 g) powdered sugar
I teaspoon vanilla extract
2 tablespoons (12 g) gluten-free cookies
  and cream cookie crumbs

FOR THE TOPPING:
Gluten-free cookies and cream cookies,
  broken into pieces

TO MAKE THE DOUGHNUTS: Preheat your oven to 350°F (180°C, or gas mark 4) and grease your doughnut pan.

Combine the oat flour, sweet rice flour, cane sugar, almond meal, baking powder, and salt in a large bowl, mixing well. In another bowl, whisk the eggs together. Then whisk in the milk, applesauce, oil, and vanilla extract.

Pour the wet mixture into the dry ingredients and stir with a large wooden spoon until just combined, being careful not to overmix (stop when you no longer see dry flour). Gently fold in the crushed cookie crumbs.

Spoon the batter into the doughnut molds, filling to just below the top of each mold, ⅛- to ¼-inch (3 to 6 mm) from the top. Bake for 18 to 22 minutes until lightly golden brown around the edges. A toothpick inserted in the center should come out clean. Let cool in the pan for 5 minutes. Slide a thin spatula around the edges of the doughnuts to help loosen them out. Then place on a cooling rack and allow to cool fully before topping.

TO MAKE THE FROSTING: Beat the butter and cream cheese together until fluffy and smooth. Slowly beat in the powdered sugar until creamy and then beat in the vanilla extract. Fold in the cookie crumbs until evenly distributed. Spread the frosting over the doughnuts and top with broken cookies.

BISCUITS AND JAM DOUGHNUTS
WITH BUTTER AND JAM TOPPING

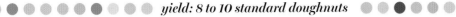

yield: 8 to 10 standard doughnuts

A super light and fluffy, buttery delicious cross between a doughnut and a drop biscuit.
With a hint of cinnamon, all this doughnut needs is a smear of butter and jam on top. It's a definite breakfast contender.

RECOMMENDED PANS:
Standard

FOR THE DOUGHNUTS:
¾ cup (90 g) oat flour
⅓ cup (47 g) sweet rice flour
¼ cup (20 g) almond meal
I teaspoon baking powder
½ teaspoon cinnamon
½ teaspoon baking soda
½ teaspoon salt
I large egg
¼ cup (60 ml) milk
¼ cup (50 g) plain Greek yogurt
¼ cup (35 g) butter, melted and
    slightly cooled
2 tablespoons (40 g) honey
I teaspoon vanilla extract

FOR THE TOPPING:
Butter, softened
Jam (or jelly)

Preheat your oven to 350°F (180°C, or gas mark 4) and grease your doughnut pan.

Combine the oat flour, sweet rice flour, almond meal, baking powder, cinnamon, baking soda, and salt in a large bowl, mixing well. In another bowl, whisk the egg. Then whisk in the milk, yogurt, butter, honey, and vanilla extract.

Pour the wet mixture into the dry ingredients and stir with a large wooden spoon until just combined, being careful not to overmix (stop when you no longer see dry flour).

Spoon the batter into the doughnut molds, filling to just below the top of each mold, ⅛- to ¼-inch (3 to 6 mm) from the top. Bake for 18 to 22 minutes until lightly golden brown around the edges. A toothpick inserted in the center should come out clean. Let cool in the pan for 5 minutes. Slide a thin spatula around the edges of the doughnuts to help loosen them out. Then place on a cooling rack and allow to cool for about 10 minutes before topping.

Top the slightly warm doughnuts with a swipe of butter and jam right before serving.

VANILLA ALMOND CAKE DOUGHNUTS
WITH HONEY ALMOND TOPPING

yield: 8 to 10 standard doughnuts

Say you like vanilla cake but sometimes you want to dress it up a bit. Well, I happen to have the dough-nut just for you. Almond extract is used to add a more complex flavor, while chocolate glaze and toasted honeyed almonds give this doughnut that little something extra you're looking for.

RECOMMENDED PANS:
Standard, mini, holes, twist

FOR THE DOUGHNUTS:
½ cup (60 g) oat flour
½ cup (70 g) sweet rice flour
⅓ cup (67 g) pure cane sugar
3 tablespoons (21 g) almond meal
1 teaspoon baking powder
½ teaspoon salt
2 large eggs
¼ cup + 2 tablespoons (88 ml) buttermilk
¼ cup (60 g) unsweetened applesauce
2 tablespoons (28 ml) oil
2 teaspoons vanilla bean paste
¾ teaspoon almond extract

FOR THE TOPPING:
¾ cup (69 g) toasted sliced almonds
1½ tablespoons (30 g) honey, warmed
Pinch of salt

FOR THE GLAZE:
1 cup (120 g) powdered sugar
3 to 4 tablespoons (45 to 60 ml) milk
½ teaspoon vanilla extract
¼ teaspoon almond extract

TO MAKE THE DOUGHNUTS: Preheat your oven to 350°F (180°C, or gas mark 4) and grease your doughnut pan.

Combine the oat flour, sweet rice flour, cane sugar, almond meal, baking powder, and salt in a large bowl, mixing well. In another bowl, whisk the eggs together. Then whisk in the buttermilk, applesauce, oil, vanilla bean paste, and almond extract.

Pour the wet mixture into the dry ingredients and stir with a large wooden spoon until just combined, being careful not to overmix (stop when you no longer see dry flour).

Spoon the batter into the doughnut molds, filling to just below the top of each mold, ⅛- to ¼-inch (3 to 6 mm) from the top. Bake for 18 to 22 minutes until lightly golden brown around the edges. A toothpick inserted in the center should come out clean. Let cool in the pan for 5 minutes. Slide a thin spatula around the edges of the doughnuts to help loosen them out. Then place on a cooling rack and allow to cool fully before topping.

TO MAKE THE NUT TOPPING: Stir the almonds and salt with the honey until combined.

TO MAKE THE GLAZE: Mix the glaze ingredients together until smooth. Add more milk if a thinner consistency is desired.

Invert the doughnut into the glaze, letting the excess drip off, or drizzle over the doughnuts. Top with nut topping and let set until the glaze has hardened.

VANILLA BEAN BIRTHDAY DOUGHNUTS
WITH VANILLA BEAN CREAM FROSTING

yield: 8 to 10 standard doughnuts

I have to admit that I like vanilla more than chocolate. I will always pick vanilla cake over chocolate cake, and when it comes to doughnuts, my feelings are the same. Like a plain cheese pizza with extra cheese, this doughnut is filled with vanilla and then topped with a vanilla bean glaze. They are perfect birthday celebration doughnuts.

RECOMMENDED PANS:
Standard, mini, holes, twist

FOR THE DOUGHNUTS:
½ cup (60 g) oat flour
½ cup (70 g) sweet rice flour
⅓ cup (67 g) pure cane sugar
3 tablespoons (21 g) almond meal
I teaspoon baking powder
½ teaspoon salt
2 large eggs
⅓ cup (80 ml) milk
¼ cup (60 g) unsweetened applesauce
2 tablespoons (28 ml) oil
2 teaspoons vanilla bean paste
⅛ teaspoon almond extract

FOR THE FROSTING:
I½ tablespoons (21 g) butter, softened
I tablespoon (15 g) cream cheese, softened
¾ to I cup (90 to 120 g) powdered sugar
I½ to 2 tablespoons (23 to 28 ml) milk
I teaspoon vanilla bean paste

FOR THE TOPPING:
Sprinkles

TO MAKE THE DOUGHNUTS: Preheat your oven to 350°F (180°C, or gas mark 4) and grease your doughnut pan.

Combine the oat flour, sweet rice flour, cane sugar, almond meal, baking powder, and salt in a large bowl, mixing well. In another bowl, whisk the eggs together. Then whisk in the milk, applesauce, oil, vanilla bean paste, and almond extract.

Pour the wet mixture into the dry ingredients and stir with a large wooden spoon until just combined, being careful not to overmix (stop when you no longer see dry flour).

Spoon the batter into the doughnut molds, filling to just below the top of each mold, ⅛- to ¼-inch (3 to 6 mm) from the top. Bake for 18 to 22 minutes until lightly golden brown around the edges. A toothpick inserted in the center should come out clean. Let cool in the pan for 5 minutes. Slide a thin spatula around the edges of the doughnuts to help loosen them out. Then place on a cooling rack and allow to cool fully before topping.

TO MAKE THE FROSTING: Beat the butter and cream cheese together until fluffy and smooth. Slowly beat in the powdered sugar until creamy and then beat in the milk and vanilla bean paste until smooth. Spread the frosting over the doughnuts and top with sprinkles.

TRES LECHES DOUGHNUTS
WITH TRES LECHES TOPPING

yield: 8 to 10 standard doughnuts

Quick! Grab a fork or maybe even a spoon! This triple-milk baked doughnut is silky soft, lightly sweetened, and begging to be drenched in a creamy milk topping. You will be licking the plate on this one. Don't say I didn't warn you.

RECOMMENDED PANS:
Standard, mini

FOR THE DOUGHNUTS:
½ cup (60 g) oat flour
½ cup (70 g) sweet rice flour
½ cup pure (100 g) cane sugar
3 tablespoons (21 g) almond meal
1 teaspoon baking powder
½ teaspoon salt
2 large eggs
¼ cup (60 ml) full-fat canned
　coconut milk, whisked
¼ cup (60 ml) 2% milk
¼ cup (60 g) unsweetened applesauce
2 tablespoons (28 ml) oil
1 tablespoon (15 ml) half-and-half
1½ teaspoons vanilla extract

FOR THE TOPPING:
1 cup (235 ml) full-fat canned
　coconut milk
½ cup (120 ml) 2% milk
¼ cup (60 ml) half-and-half
3 tablespoons (60 g) honey

TO MAKE THE DOUGHNUTS: Preheat your oven to 350°F (180°C, or gas mark 4) and grease your doughnut pan.

Combine the oat flour, sweet rice flour, cane sugar, almond meal, baking powder, and salt in a large bowl, mixing well. In another bowl, whisk the eggs together. Then whisk in the coconut milk, 2% milk, applesauce, oil, half-and-half, and vanilla extract.

Pour the wet mixture into the dry ingredients and stir with a large wooden spoon until just combined, being careful not to overmix (stop when you no longer see dry flour).

Spoon the batter into the doughnut molds, filling to just below the top of each mold, $1/8$- to ¼-inch (3 to 6 mm) from the top. Bake for 18 to 22 minutes until lightly golden brown around the edges. A toothpick inserted in the center should come out clean. Let cool in the pan for 5 minutes. Slide a thin spatula around the edges of the doughnuts to help loosen them out. Then place on a cooling rack and allow to cool fully before topping.

TO MAKE THE TOPPING: Whisk the topping ingredients until fully combined. Place each doughnut on a plate and pour the milk topping over the doughnuts just before serving.

TIRAMISU DOUGHNUTS
WITH KAHLÚA MASCARPONE FROSTING

yield: 8 to 10 standard doughnuts

A note from my good friend, David: "Tasters of this treat will delight in the harmonious aromas of espresso, cocoa, coffee liqueur, and the fact that the description for tiramisu will no longer involve the use of the awkward term 'ladyfingers'." I couldn't have said it better myself. Thanks, David!

RECOMMENDED PANS:
Standard, mini, holes, twist

FOR THE DOUGHNUTS:
½ cup (60 g) oat flour
½ cup (70 g) sweet rice flour
⅓ cup (67 g) pure cane sugar
¼ cup (28 g) almond meal
2½ teaspoons (3 g) instant espresso
    powder
I teaspoon baking powder
½ teaspoon salt
2 large eggs
⅓ cup (80 ml) milk
3 tablespoons (45 g) unsweetened
    applesauce
2 tablespoons (28 ml) oil
2 teaspoons vanilla bean paste
¼ cup (60 g) mascarpone cheese,
    softened

FOR THE SYRUP:
¼ cup (60 ml) brewed espresso
1½ tablespoons (23 ml) Kahlúa
I tablespoon (20 g) honey

FOR THE FROSTING:
½ cup (120 g) mascarpone cheese
¼ cup + 2 tablespoons (45 g) powdered
    sugar
2 to 3 tablespoons (28 to 45 ml) Kahlúa
Cocoa powder to dust on top

TO MAKE THE DOUGHNUTS: Preheat your oven to 350°F (180°C, or gas mark 4) and grease your doughnut pan.

Combine the oat flour, sweet rice flour, cane sugar, almond meal, instant espresso powder, baking powder, and salt in a large bowl, mixing well. In another bowl, whisk the eggs together. Then whisk in the milk, applesauce, oil, and vanilla bean paste. Vigorously whisk in the mascarpone cheese until broken apart and evenly distributed. The mixture will not be completely smooth.

Pour the wet mixture into the dry ingredients and stir with a large wooden spoon until just combined, being careful not to overmix (stop when you no longer see dry flour).

Spoon the batter into the doughnut molds, filling just below the top of each mold, ⅛- to ¼-inch (3 to 6 mm) from the top. Bake for 18 to 22 minutes until lightly golden brown around the edges. A toothpick inserted in the center should come out clean. Let cool in the pan for 5 minutes. Slide a thin spatula around the edges of the doughnuts to help loosen them out. Then place on a cooling rack and allow to cool fully before topping.

TO MAKE THE SYRUP: Whisk together the espresso, Kahlúa, and honey in a small bowl until the espresso is dissolved. Brush 3 or 4 coats over top of each doughnut right before frosting.

TO MAKE THE FROSTING: Beat the mascarpone and powdered sugar together until smooth. Beat in the Kahlúa. Gently spread the frosting over each doughnut. Dust with sifted cocoa powder to finish.

BAKLAVA DOUGHNUTS
WITH HONEY BUTTER TRIPLE NUT TOPPING

yield: 8 to 10 standard doughnuts

This doughnut will satisfy all of your baklava cravings without having to fuss over layers and layers of fragile phyllo dough. And not only are these doughnuts filled with a honey butter nut mixture, but they're topped with one, too.

RECOMMENDED PANS:
Standard, twist

FOR THE NUT MIXTURE:
¼ cup + 2 tablespoons (120 g) honey
¼ cup (55 g) butter, melted
1½ teaspoons vanilla extract
1 teaspoon cinnamon
¼ teaspoon ground cloves
¼ teaspoon salt
½ cup (62 g) roasted pistachios
½ cup unsalted (50 g) roasted pecans
½ cup (50 g) roasted walnuts

FOR THE DOUGHNUTS:
½ cup (60 g) oat flour
½ cup (70 g) sweet rice flour
3 tablespoons (21 g) almond meal
2 tablespoons (26 g) pure cane sugar
1 teaspoon baking powder
½ teaspoon cinnamon
½ teaspoon salt
2 large eggs
⅓ cup (80 ml) milk
¼ cup (60 g) unsweetened applesauce
3 tablespoons (60 g) honey
2 tablespoons (28 g) butter, melted and
   lightly cooled
1½ teaspoons vanilla extract

FOR THE TOPPING:
½ cup (160 g) honey
2 tablespoons (28 g) butter, softened

TO MAKE THE NUT MIXTURE: Whisk the honey, butter, vanilla extract, cinnamon, clove, and salt together in a bowl. Stir in the roasted nuts until combined. Set aside.

TO MAKE THE DOUGHNUTS: Preheat your oven to 350°F (180°C, or gas mark 4) and grease your doughnut pan.

Combine the oat flour, sweet rice flour, almond meal, cane sugar, baking powder, cinnamon, and salt in a large bowl, mixing well. In another bowl, whisk the eggs together. Then whisk in the milk, applesauce, honey, butter, and vanilla extract.

Pour the wet mixture into the dry and stir with a large wooden spoon until just combined, being careful not to overmix (stop when you no longer see dry flour).

Spoon the batter into the doughnut molds, filling just halfway. Sprinkle about 1 tablespoon (8 g) of the nut mixture around each doughnut and cover with the remaining batter to just below the top of each mold, ⅛- to ¼-inch (3 to 6 mm) from the top. Bake for 18 to 22 minutes until lightly golden brown around the edges. A toothpick inserted in the center should come out clean. Let cool in the pan for 5 minutes. Slide a thin spatula around the edges of the doughnuts to help loosen them out. Then place on a cooling rack and allow to cool fully before topping.

TO MAKE THE TOPPING: In a small pot over medium-low heat, bring the honey to a simmer, whisking constantly. Turn off the heat and pour in a shallow bowl. Whisk in the butter until smooth. Carefully dip the top of the doughnut in the honey butter and let the excess drip off. Top each doughnut with the remaining nut mixture and let cool before serving. Drizzle more of the honey butter on top if desired.

RED VELVET DOUGHNUTS
WITH CREAM CHEESE FROSTING

yield: 8 to 10 standard doughnuts

You may be surprised when you see the ingredient list below and notice it calls for beet purée. Fear not. These doughnuts do not taste like beets. They're used to give a lovely and natural red hue in this classic red velvet flavor. With a hint of chocolate, a soft and fluffy texture, and a super-smooth cream cheese frosting, I promise you these won't last long.

RECOMMENDED PANS:
Standard, mini, holes, twist

FOR THE BEET PURÉE:
2 large red beets, peeled
1 tablespoon (15 ml) lemon juice
2 to 4 tablespoons (28 to 60 ml) buttermilk

FOR THE DOUGHNUTS:
½ cup (60 g) oat flour
½ cup (70 g) sweet rice flour
2 tablespoons (14 g) almond meal
½ cup (100 g) pure cane sugar
1 tablespoon (5 g) unsweetened cocoa powder
1 teaspoon baking powder
½ teaspoon salt
2 large eggs
6 tablespoons (90 ml) buttermilk
3 tablespoons (45 g) beet purée
3 tablespoons (45 g) unsweetened applesauce
2 tablespoons (28 ml) oil
2 teaspoons vanilla extract

FOR THE FROSTING:
¼ cup (60 g) cream cheese, softened
1 tablespoon (14 g) butter, softened
½ cup (60 g) powdered sugar
2 to 4 tablespoons (28 to 60 ml) half-and-half
½ teaspoon vanilla exract
Sprinkles, to top

TO MAKE THE PURÉE: Preheat your oven to 375°F (190°C, or gas mark 5). Wrap beets in foil and place on a baking sheet for about 45 minutes to 1 hour, or until fork-tender. Or chop and steam until fully tender. Let cool.

Place beets in a high-speed blender with the lemon juice and 2 tablespoons (28 ml) buttermilk. Purée until smooth and about the thickness of applesauce. Add more buttermilk as needed. Measure 3 tablespoons (45 ml) of buttermilk to be added to the batter.

TO MAKE THE DOUGHNUTS: Preheat your oven to 350°F (180°C, or gas mark 4) and grease your doughnut pan.

Combine the oat flour, sweet rice flour, almond meal, cane sugar, cocoa powder, baking powder, and salt in a large bowl, mixing well. In another bowl, whisk the eggs together. Then whisk in the buttermilk, beet purée, applesauce, oil, and vanilla extract.

Pour the wet mixture into the dry ingredients and stir with a large wooden spoon until just combined, being careful not to overmix (stop when you no longer see dry flour).

Spoon the batter into the doughnut molds, filling to just below the top of each mold, ⅛- to ¼-inch (3 to 6 mm) from the top. Bake for 18 to 22 minutes until lightly golden brown around the edges. A toothpick inserted in the center should come out clean. Let cool in the pan for 5 minutes. Slide a thin spatula around the edges of the doughnuts to help loosen them out. Then place on a cooling rack and allow to cool fully before topping.

TO MAKE THE FROSTING: Beat the cream cheese and butter together until fluffy and smooth. Beat in the powdered sugar until smooth and then beat in the half-and-half and vanilla extract. The frosting should be soft and spreadable. Spread the frosting over the doughnuts and top with sprinkles.

CHAPTER 6

decadent indulgences

FOR THE ULTIMATE SWEET LOVER.

· ·

Watch out! You may need a fork and knife to enter this chapter. Things are going to get a little messy, which I'm hoping you're okay with. The recipes you'll find are sweet, stuffed, and packed with every topping combination you can think of. From fragrant vanilla beans to rich chocolate, these recipes are for the ultimate sweet lover.

· ·

BROWN SUGAR CARAMEL DOUGHNUTS
WITH SEA SALT CARAMEL GLAZE

 *yield: 8 to 10 standard doughnuts*

Not only have I always been a vanilla lover, but caramel is my all-time favorite candy filling. I've turned this caramel into a glaze, and when combined with a sprinkle of sea salt, your brain and mouth may just explode. Mine sure did.

RECOMMENDED PANS:
Standard, mini, holes, twist

FOR THE DOUGHNUTS:
½ cup (60 g) oat flour
½ cup (70 g) sweet rice flour
⅓ cup (75 g) packed dark brown sugar
3 tablespoons (19 g) almond meal
1 teaspoon baking powder
½ teaspoon salt
¼ teaspoon cinnamon
2 large eggs
⅓ cup (80 ml) milk
¼ cup (60 g) unsweetened applesauce
2 tablespoons (28 ml) oil
1 tablespoon (20 g) pure maple syrup
2 teaspoons vanilla bean paste

FOR THE GLAZE:
¼ cup (60 ml) heavy cream
¼ cup (60 g) packed dark brown sugar
3 tablespoons (42 g) butter
2 tablespoons (40 g) pure maple syrup
½ scraped vanilla bean
⅓ to ½ cup (40 to 60 g) powdered sugar

FOR THE TOPPING:
Large flaked sea salt

TO MAKE THE DOUGHNUTS: Preheat your oven to 350°F (180°C, or gas mark 4) and grease your doughnut pan.

Combine the oat flour, sweet rice flour, brown sugar, almond meal, baking powder, salt, and cinnamon in a large bowl, mixing well. In another bowl, whisk the eggs together. Then whisk in the milk, applesauce, oil, maple syrup, and vanilla bean paste.

Pour the wet mixture into the dry ingredients and stir with a large wooden spoon until just combined, being careful not to overmix (stop when you no longer see dry flour).

Spoon the batter into the doughnut molds, filling to just below the top of each mold, ⅛- to ¼-inch (3 to 6 mm) from the top. Bake for 18 to 22 minutes until lightly golden brown around the edges. A toothpick inserted in the center should come out clean. Let cool in the pan for 5 minutes. Slide a thin spatula around the edges of the doughnuts to help loosen them out. Then place on a cooling rack and allow to cool fully before topping.

TO MAKE THE GLAZE: In a saucepan over medium heat, stir the cream, brown sugar, butter, maple syrup, and vanilla beans constantly until it comes to a roaring boil. Continue to boil for 1 minute, stirring constantly. Remove from the heat and let cool for 3 to 5 minutes.

Whisk in ⅓ cup (40 g) powdered sugar until smooth and pour into a small bowl. Add more powdered sugar if a thicker consistency is desired or more cream if you need to thin it out a bit.

Invert the doughnut into the glaze, letting the excess drip off, or drizzle over the doughnuts. Top with a sprinkle of sea salt. Let set until the glaze has hardened.

CHOCOLATE-COVERED STRAWBERRY DOUGHNUT
WITH STRAWBERRIES, CHOCOLATE, AND TOASTED COCONUT

● ● ● ● ● ● ● ● ● ● ● ● ● ● ● *yield: 8 to 10 standard doughnuts* ● ● ● ● ● ● ● ● ● ● ● ● ●

First, grab a fork. Second, get ready to make a huge mess while eating this loaded doughnut. Because what's better than a chocolate-covered strawberry? That's right—a strawberry chocolate-covered doughnut.

RECOMMENDED PANS:
Standard, holes, twist

FOR THE ROASTED STRAWBERRIES:
3 tablespoons (60 g) honey
I tablespoon (15 ml) balsamic vinegar
2 tablespoons (28 ml) melted coconut oil
¼ teaspoon salt
2 pints (24 ounces, or 680 g) strawberries, hulled and quartered

FOR THE TOASTED COCONUT:
½ cup (40 g) flaked unsweetened coconut, toasted

FOR THE DOUGHNUTS:
½ cup (60 g) oat flour
½ cup (70 g) sweet rice flour
¼ cup + 2 tablespoons (76 g) pure cane sugar
¼ cup (20 g) unsweetened cocoa powder
¼ cup (28 g) almond meal
I teaspoon baking powder
½ teaspoon salt
2 large eggs
⅓ cup (80 ml) milk
3 tablespoons (45 g) applesauce
2 tablespoons (28 ml) oil
1½ teaspoons vanilla extract
⅓ cup (56 g) roasted strawberries

FOR THE DRIZZLE:
I cup (175 g) dark chocolate chips
I tablespoon (14 g) coconut oil

TO MAKE THE ROASTED STRAWBERRIES: Preheat your oven to 375°F (190°C, or gas mark 5) and line a large rimmed baking sheet with parchment paper.

Whisk together the honey, vinegar, oil, and salt in a small bowl. Toss with the strawberries and spread on pan. Roast about 25 minutes until tender and caramelized. Let cool fully. Measure out ⅓ cup (56 g) to add to the batter and use the rest as a topping.

TO MAKE THE TOASTED COCONUT: Preheat your oven to 350°F (180°C, or gas mark 4) and place the flaked coconut in a single layer on a baking sheet. Toast for 5 to 10 minutes, stirring once or twice, until evenly golden brown. Watch closely.

TO MAKE THE DOUGHNUTS: Leave the oven on for the doughnuts. Grease your doughnut pan.

Combine the dry ingredients in a large bowl, mixing well. In another bowl, whisk the eggs together. Then whisk in the milk, applesauce, oil, and vanilla extract.

Pour the wet mixture into the dry ingredients and stir with a large wooden spoon until just combined, being careful not to overmix. Gently fold the roasted strawberries into the batter.

Spoon the batter into the doughnut molds, filling to just below the top of each mold, ⅛- to ¼-inch (3 to 6 mm) from the top. Bake for 20 to 24 minutes until lightly golden brown around the edges. A toothpick inserted in the center should come out clean. Let cool in the pan for 5 minutes. Slide a thin spatula around the edges of the doughnuts to help loosen them out. Then place on a cooling rack and allow to cool fully before icing.

TO MAKE THE DRIZZLE: Melt the chocolate chips and coconut oil in a double boiler, stirring until smooth, or place in a small microwave-safe bowl and microwave for 30-second increments, stirring after each interval, until smooth. Drizzle over the dough-nuts. Top with roasted strawberries and toasted coconut and serve immediately.

CHOCOLATE MACAROON DOUGHNUTS
WITH CHOCOLATE COCONUT SHELL TOPPING

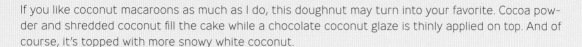

yield: 10 to 12 standard doughnuts

If you like coconut macaroons as much as I do, this doughnut may turn into your favorite. Cocoa powder and shredded coconut fill the cake while a chocolate coconut glaze is thinly applied on top. And of course, it's topped with more snowy white coconut.

RECOMMENDED PANS:
Standard, mini, holes, twist

FOR THE DOUGHNUTS:
½ cup (60 g) oat flour
½ cup (70 g) sweet rice flour
3 tablespoons (21 g) almond meal
¼ cup (20 g) unsweetened cocoa
   powder
¾ cup (60 g) unsweetened shredded
   coconut
I teaspoon baking powder
½ teaspoon salt
2 large eggs
½ cup + 2 tablespoons (148 ml) milk
¼ cup (60 g) unsweetened applesauce
2 tablespoons (28 ml) oil
I½ teaspoons vanilla extract

FOR THE TOPPING:
¾ cup (131 g) dark chocolate chips
¼ cup (55 g) coconut butter
Unsweetened shredded coconut

TO MAKE THE DOUGHNUTS: Preheat your oven to 350°F (180°C, or gas mark 4) and grease your doughnut pan.

Combine the oat flour, sweet rice flour, almond meal, cocoa powder, coconut, baking powder, and salt in a bowl, mixing well. In another bowl, whisk the eggs together. Then whisk in the milk, applesauce, oil, and vanilla extract.

Pour the wet mixture into the dry ingredients and stir with a large wooden spoon until just combined, being careful not to overmix (stop when you no longer see dry flour).

Spoon the batter into the doughnut molds filling to just below the top of each mold, ⅛- to ¼-inch (3 to 6 mm) from the top. Bake for 18 to 22 minutes until lightly golden brown around the edges. A toothpick inserted in the center should come out clean. Let cool in the pan for 5 minutes. Slide a thin spatula around the edges of the doughnuts to help loosen them out. Then place on a cooling rack and allow to cool fully before topping.

TO MAKE THE TOPPING: Melt the chocolate and coconut butter in a double boiler, stirring until smooth, or microwave for 30-second intervals, stirring after each interval until the mixture is smooth. Invert doughnuts into the coating, let the excess drip off, or drizzle over the doughnuts. Top with shredded coconut and let set until the topping has hardened.

CHOCOLATE CANDY CANE DOUGHNUTS
WITH CHOCOLATE GLAZE AND CRUSHED CANDY CANES

yield: 8 to 10 standard doughnuts

Here's a rich, dark chocolaty doughnut, topped with a sweet, chocolate glaze and finished with a peppermint crunch. These doughnuts are festive around the holidays and will definitely help you get your chocolate peppermint fix for the year. This is one of my all-time favorite flavor combinations!

RECOMMENDED PANS:
Standard, mini, holes, twist

FOR THE DOUGHNUTS:
½ cup (60 g) oat flour
½ cup (70 g) sweet rice flour
½ cup pure (100 g) cane sugar
¼ cup (20 g) unsweetened cocoa
   powder
3 tablespoons (21 g) almond meal
1 teaspoon baking powder
½ teaspoon salt
2 large eggs
½ cup (120 ml) milk
¼ cup (60 g) unsweetened applesauce
2 tablespoons (28 ml) oil
1 teaspoon vanilla extract
½ teaspoon peppermint extract

FOR THE GLAZE:
1 cup (120 g) powdered sugar
4 to 6 tablespoons (60 to 90 ml) milk
3 tablespoons (15 g) unsweetened cocoa
   powder

FOR THE TOPPING:
Crushed candy canes

TO MAKE THE DOUGHNUTS: Preheat your oven to 350°F (180°C, or gas mark 4) and grease your doughnut pan.

Combine the oat flour, sweet rice flour, cane sugar, cocoa powder, almond meal, baking powder, and salt in a bowl, mixing well. In another bowl, whisk the eggs together. Then whisk in the milk, applesauce, oil, vanilla extract, and peppermint extract.

Pour the wet mixture into the dry ingredients and stir with a large wooden spoon until just combined, being careful not to overmix (stop when you no longer see dry flour).

Spoon the batter into the doughnut molds, filling to just below the top of each mold, $\frac{1}{8}$- to ¼-inch (3 to 6 mm) from the top. Bake for 18 to 22 minutes until lightly golden brown around the edges. A toothpick inserted in the center should come out clean. Let cool in the pan for 5 minutes. Slide a thin spatula around the edges of the doughnuts to help loosen them out. Then place on a cooling rack and allow to cool fully before topping.

TO MAKE THE GLAZE: Mix the glaze ingredients together until smooth. Add more milk for a thinner consistency. Invert doughnuts into the coating, letting the excess drip off, or drizzle over the doughnuts. Top with crushed candy canes and let set until the glaze has hardened.

HAZELNUT DOUGHNUTS
WITH CHOCOLATE HAZELNUT GLAZE AND ROASTED HAZELNUTS

yield: 8 to 10 standard doughnuts

Raise your hand if you're in love with that oh-so-popular creamy, chocolate hazelnut spread known as Nutella. All of you? That's what I expected. The doughnut is lightly flavored with chocolate, vanilla, and hazelnut, then finished with a rich glaze and crunchy nut topping.

RECOMMENDED PANS:
Standard, mini, holes, twist

FOR THE DOUGHNUTS:
½ cup (60 g) oat flour
½ cup (70 g) sweet rice flour
¼ cup (28 g) roasted hazelnut meal or almond meal
I teaspoon baking powder
½ teaspoon salt
2 large eggs
¼ cup + 2 tablespoons (88 ml) milk
3 tablespoons (45 g) unsweetened applesauce
2 tablespoons (28 ml) oil
I tablespoon (I6 g) chocolate hazelnut spread
2 teaspoons vanilla bean paste

FOR THE GLAZE:
¾ cup (90 g) powdered sugar
4½ tablespoons (72 g) chocolate hazelnut spread
3 to 5 tablespoons (45 to 75 ml) milk

FOR THE TOPPING:
Roasted chopped hazelnuts

TO MAKE THE DOUGHNUTS: Preheat your oven to 350°F (I80°C, or gas mark 4) and grease your doughnut pan.

Combine the oat flour, sweet rice flour, hazelnut meal, baking powder, and salt in a bowl, mixing well. In another bowl, whisk the eggs together. Then whisk in the milk, applesauce, oil, chocolate hazelnut spread, and vanilla bean paste.

Pour the wet mixture into the dry ingredients and stir with a large wooden spoon until just combined, being careful not to overmix (stop when you no longer see dry flour).

Spoon the batter into the doughnut molds, filling to just below the top of each mold, $1/8$- to ¼-inch (3 to 6 mm) from the top. Bake for I8 to 22 minutes until lightly golden brown around the edges. A toothpick inserted in the center should come out clean. Let cool in the pan for 5 minutes. Slide a thin spatula around the edges of the doughnuts to help loosen them out. Then place on a cooling rack and allow to cool fully before topping.

TO MAKE THE GLAZE: Mix the powdered sugar and chocolate hazelnut spread together until smooth. Mix in the milk, adding more for a thinner consistency.

Invert doughnuts into the coating, letting the excess drip off, or drizzle over the doughnuts. Top with chopped hazelnuts and let set until the glaze has hardened.

TRIPLE CHOCOLATE DOUGHNUTS
WITH DARK CHOCOLATE CREAM FROSTING

● *yield: 10 to 12 standard doughnuts* ●

Chocolate doughnut. Chocolate chips. Chocolate frosting. Death by chocolate? I think so. These are a chocolate lover's dream.

RECOMMENDED PANS:
Standard, mini, holes, twist

FOR THE DOUGHNUTS:
½ cup (60 g) oat flour
½ cup (70 g) sweet rice flour
½ cup (100 g) pure cane sugar
¼ cup (20 g) unsweetened cocoa powder
3 tablespoons (21 g) almond meal
1 teaspoon baking powder
½ teaspoon salt
2 large eggs
½ cup (120 ml) milk
¼ cup (60 g) applesauce
2 tablespoons (28 ml) oil
2 teaspoons vanilla extract
½ cup (88 g) dark chocolate chips

FOR THE FROSTING:
2 to 3 tablespoons (28 to 45 ml) heavy cream or milk
⅔ cup (80 g) powdered sugar
3 tablespoons (42 g) butter, softened
¼ cup (20 g) unsweetened cocoa powder

TO MAKE THE DOUGHNUTS: Preheat your oven to 350°F (180°C, or gas mark 4) and grease your doughnut pan.

Combine the oat flour, sweet rice flour, cane sugar, cocoa powder, almond meal, baking powder, and salt in a large bowl, mixing well. In another bowl, whisk the eggs together. Then whisk in the milk, applesauce, oil, and vanilla extract.

Pour the wet mixture into the dry ingredients and stir with a large wooden spoon until just combined, being careful not to overmix (stop when you no longer see dry flour). Gently fold the dark chocolate chips into the batter.

Spoon the batter into the doughnut molds, filling to just below the top of each mold, ⅛- to ¼-inch (3 to 6 mm) from the top. Bake for 18 to 22 minutes until lightly golden brown around the edges. A toothpick inserted in the center should come out clean. Let cool in the pan for 5 minutes. Slide a thin spatula around the edges of the doughnuts to help loosen them out. Then place on a cooling rack and allow to cool fully before icing.

TO MAKE THE FROSTING: Mix the frosting ingredients together until fully combined and smooth. Add more milk if needed.

Spread the chocolate frosting on the doughnuts.

RECIPE NOTE

After spreading the doughnuts with chocolate frosting, feel free to top them with sprinkles, chopped chocolate chips, coconut, chocolate candy, or your favorite nut.

SWEET POTATO PECAN PIE DOUGHNUTS
WITH ROASTED PECAN CRUNCH TOPPING

● ● ● ● ● ● ● ● ● ● ● ● ● ● ● *yield: 10 to 12 standard doughnuts* ● ● ● ● ● ● ● ● ● ● ● ● ● ●

It's a doughnut! It's a pie! It's both! This sweet potato–filled doughnut is finished with a sweet pecan topping sure to make your taste buds do a happy dance.

RECOMMENDED PANS:
Standard, mini, twist

FOR THE DOUGHNUTS:
½ cup (60 g) oat flour
½ cup (70 g) sweet rice flour
¼ cup (28 g) pecan meal
2 tablespoons (26 g) pure cane sugar
I teaspoon baking powder
1½ teaspoons cinnamon
½ teaspoon salt
¼ teaspoon ground nutmeg
⅛ teaspoon ground ginger
2 large eggs
¼ cup + 2 tablespoons (88 ml) milk
⅓ cup (75 g) sweet potato purée
¼ cup (80 g) pure maple syrup
2 tablespoons (30 g) unsweetened
   applesauce
2 tablespoons (28 ml) oil
1½ teaspoons vanilla extract

FOR THE TOPPING:
½ cup (160 g) pure maple syrup
3 tablespoons (42 g) butter, melted
¼ cup (60 g) loosely packed brown sugar
½ teaspoon cinnamon
I cup (110 g) coarsely ground roasted
   pecans

TO MAKE THE DOUGHNUTS: Preheat your oven to 350°F (180°C, or gas mark 4) and grease your doughnut pan.

Combine the oat flour, sweet rice flour, pecan meal, cane sugar, baking powder, cinnamon, salt, nutmeg, and ginger in a large bowl, mixing well. In another bowl, whisk the eggs together. Then whisk in the milk, sweet potato purée, maple syrup, applesauce, oil, and vanilla extract.

Pour the wet mixture into the dry ingredients and stir with a large wooden spoon until just combined, being careful not to overmix (stop when you no longer see dry flour).

Spoon the batter into the doughnut molds, filling to just below the top of each mold, ⅛- to ¼-inch (3 to 6 mm) from the top. Bake for 18 to 22 minutes until lightly golden brown around the edges. A toothpick inserted in the center should come out clean. Let cool in the pan for 5 minutes. Slide a thin spatula around the edges of the doughnuts to help loosen them out. Then place on a cooling rack and allow to cool fully before topping.

TO MAKE THE TOPPING: In a bowl, mix the maple syrup and butter together. In another bowl, mix together the sugar, cinnamon, and ground pecans.

Brush each doughnut with a light coating of the butter mixture and sprinkle the pecan mixture over top. Drizzle each doughnut with the remaining butter mixture to help the pecan mixture stick. Let the doughnuts rest for 10 to 15 minutes and then serve.

RECIPE NOTE

Pecan meal can be made at home by following the same instructions for making almond meal on page II. Be sure to use raw pecans.

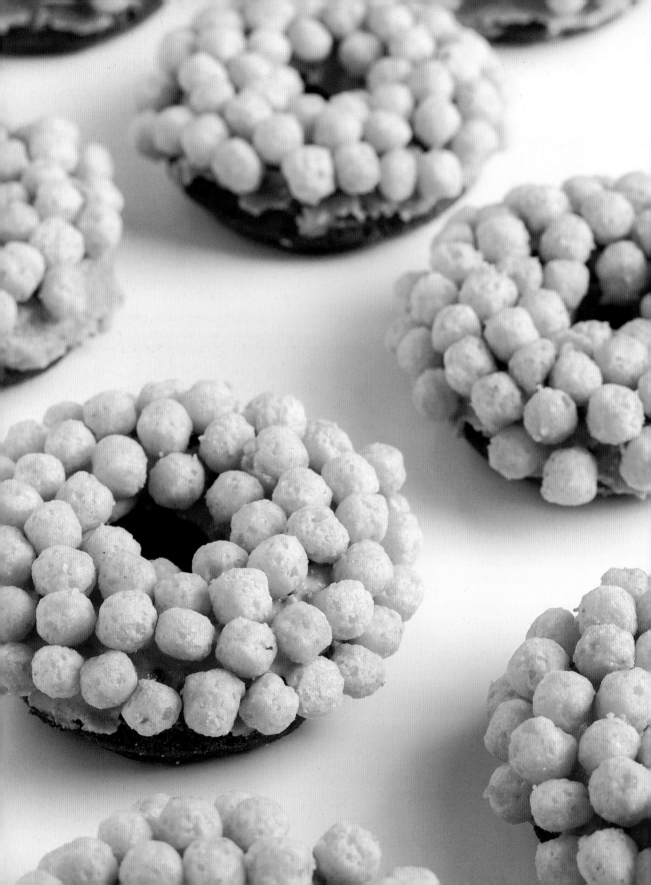

PEANUT BUTTER CRUNCH DOUGHNUTS
WITH PEANUT BUTTER FROSTING AND PEANUT BUTTER CEREAL

yield: 10 to 12 standard doughnuts

If you like peanut butter, this doughnut will be calling your name. It's fully loaded with peanut butter from the cake doughnut, to the frosting, to the peanut butter crunch topping. But just in case that's not enticing enough, these doughnuts are packed with chocolate as well! It's an irresistible doughnut for the kids, or the kid in you.

RECOMMENDED PANS:
Standard, mini

FOR THE DOUGHNUTS:
½ cup (60 g) oat flour
½ cup (70 g) sweet rice flour
½ cup (100 g) pure cane sugar
¼ cup (20 g) unsweetened cocoa powder
3 tablespoons (21 g) peanut meal (page 83)
1 teaspoon baking powder
½ teaspoon salt
2 large eggs
½ cup (60 ml) milk
¼ cup (60 g) unsweetened applesauce
2 tablespoons (32 g) creamy peanut butter, melted and slightly cooled
2 tablespoons (28 ml) oil
1½ teaspoons vanilla extract
½ cup (88 g) dark chocolate chips

FOR THE FROSTING:
1 cup (260 g) creamy peanut butter
¼ cup (30 g) powdered sugar
1½ tablespoons (30 g) honey
⅛ teaspoon salt

FOR THE TOPPING:
Gluten-free peanut butter cereal

TO MAKE THE DOUGHNUTS: Preheat your oven to 350°F (180°C, or gas mark 4) and grease your doughnut pan.

Combine the oat flour, sweet rice flour, cane sugar, cocoa powder, peanut meal, baking powder, and salt in a large bowl, mixing well. In another bowl, whisk the eggs together. Then whisk in the milk, applesauce, peanut butter, oil, and vanilla extract.

Pour the wet mixture into the dry ingredients and stir with a large wooden spoon until just combined, being careful not to overmix (stop when you no longer see dry flour). Gently fold in the chocolate chips.

Spoon the batter into the doughnut molds, filling to just below the top of each mold, ⅛- to ¼-inch (3 to 6 mm) from the top. Bake for 18 to 22 minutes until lightly golden brown around the edges. A toothpick inserted in the center should come out clean. Let cool in the pan for 5 minutes. Slide a thin spatula around the edges of the doughnuts to help loosen them out. Then place on a cooling rack and allow to cool fully before topping.

TO MAKE THE FROSTING: Beat the peanut butter and powdered sugar together until smooth and creamy. Beat in the honey and salt. Spread on the cooled doughnuts.

Place the cereal in a bowl and invert the frosted doughnut into the bowl, pressing lightly. Lift up and fill in any blank spots with more cereal.

APPLE PIE DOUGHNUTS
WITH APPLE PIE FILLING, WHIPPED CREAM, AND CARAMEL

yield: 8 to 10 doughnuts

I'm overly excited for this recipe. It starts with a thinner-than-normal doughnut that gets sliced in half. The two halves are then used as the bottom and top crust, which are filled with a quick-cooked apple pie filling. Just don't forget the whipped cream and caramel toppings!

RECOMMENDED PANS:
Standard

FOR THE DOUGHNUTS:
⅓ cup (40 g) oat flour
⅓ cup (47 g) sweet rice flour
⅓ cup (34 g) blanched almond flour
¼ cup (50 g) pure cane sugar
1 teaspoon baking powder
¼ teaspoon salt
2 large eggs
¼ cup (60 ml) milk
3 tablespoons (45 g) unsweetened applesauce
3 tablespoons (42 g) butter, melted and slightly cooled
1 teaspoon vanilla extract

FOR THE FILLING:
½ cup (160 g) pure maple syrup
¼ cup (55 g) butter
1 tablespoon (8 g) arrowroot starch or cornstarch
1 teaspoon vanilla extract
1½ teaspoons cinnamon
¼ to ½ teaspoon ginger
¼ teaspoon salt
6 cups (900 g) diced apple

FOR THE TOPPING:
Whipped cream
Caramel

TO MAKE THE DOUGHNUTS: Preheat your oven to 350°F (180°C, or gas mark 4) and grease your doughnut pan.

Combine the oat flour, sweet rice flour, almond flour, cane sugar, baking powder, and salt in a large bowl, mixing well. In another bowl, whisk the eggs together. Then whisk in the milk, applesauce, butter, and vanilla extract.

Pour the wet mixture into the dry ingredients and stir with a large wooden spoon until just combined, being careful not to overmix (stop when you no longer see dry flour).

Spoon the batter into the doughnut molds, filling up just halfway. Bake for 12 to 15 minutes until lightly golden brown around the edges. A toothpick inserted in the center should come out clean. Let cool in the pan for 5 minutes. Slide a thin spatula around the edges of the doughnuts to help loosen them out. Then place on a cooling rack and allow to cool fully before topping. Carefully slice each doughnut in half.

TO MAKE THE FILLING: In a large pot over medium heat, whisk the maple syrup, butter, arrowroot starch, vanilla extract, cinnamon, ginger, and salt together until combined. Add in the apples and stir for 5 to 7 minutes until the sauce is thickened and the apples are just starting to soften. Let cool slightly before topping the doughnuts. The mixture will thicken as it sits.

Place one doughnut half on a plate and spoon some of the apple topping over it. Then cover with the other half and add whipped cream and caramel. Serve immediately.

VEGAN GOOEY CHOCOLATE DOUGHNUTS
WITH CHOCOLATE GLAZE AND ICE CREAM TOPPING

yield: 8 to 10 standard doughnuts

Imagine a doughnut filled with chocolate, chocolate chips, and a gooey center. A chocolate explosion in your mouth. Because this recipe is vegan and doesn't include eggs, I don't blame you one bit if you lick the mixing bowl clean. Just be sure to serve this à la mode with a scoop of your favorite coconut milk ice cream.

RECOMMENDED PANS:
Standard

FOR THE DOUGHNUTS:
½ cup (60 g) oat flour
½ cup (70 g) sweet rice flour
¼ cup (20 g) unsweetened cocoa powder
¼ cup (50 g) pure cane sugar
2 tablespoons (14 g) coconut flour
1½ tablespoons (11 g) ground flax meal
1 teaspoon baking powder
½ teaspoon baking soda
½ teaspoon salt
¾ cup (175 ml) unsweetened almond milk
¼ cup + 2 tablespoons (129 g) brown rice syrup
¼ cup (60 g) pumpkin purée
2 tablespoon (28 ml) oil
2 teaspoons vanilla extract
½ cup (88 g) vegan dark chocolate chips

FOR THE GLAZE:
⅔ cup (80 g) powdered sugar
5 tablespoons (70 g) unrefined coconut oil, melted
3½ tablespoons (18 g) unsweetened cocoa powder

FOR TOPPING:
Vegan ice cream

TO MAKE THE DOUGHNUTS: Preheat your oven to 350°F (180°C, or gas mark 4) and grease your doughnut pan.

Combine the oat flour, sweet rice flour, cocoa powder, cane sugar, coconut flour, flax meal, baking powder, baking soda, and salt in a large bowl, mixing well. In another bowl, whisk together the milk, brown rice syrup, pumpkin purée, oil, and vanilla extract until well combined.

Pour the wet mixture into the dry ingredients and stir with a large wooden spoon until just combined, being careful not to overmix (stop when you no longer see dry flour). Gently fold in the chocolate chips. The mixture will be thick.

Spoon the batter into the doughnut molds, filling to just below the top of each mold, ⅛- to ¼-inch (3 to 6 mm) from the top. Bake for 20 to 26 minutes until lightly golden brown around the edges. The cake is supposed to have a gooey center. Let cool in the pan for 5 minutes. Slide a thin spatula around the edges of the doughnuts to help loosen them out. Then place on a cooling rack and allow to cool for 5 to 10 minutes before glazing.

TO MAKE THE GLAZE: Mix the powdered sugar and coconut oil together until smooth. Stir in the cocoa powder until combined. Invert the doughnut into the glaze and let the excess drip off. Serve warm, topped with ice cream.

SWEET POTATO FRITTER DOUGHNUTS
WITH CRISPY CINNAMON-SUGAR COATING

● *yield: 10 to 12 standard doughnuts* ●

This fried-tasting, not-fried doughnut is filled with cinnamon maple roasted sweet potatoes and coated with a crunchy, buttery cinnamon-sugar topping. Do I need to convince you further?

RECOMMENDED PANS:
Standard, holes, twist

FOR THE ROASTED POTATOES:
I medium sweet potato or yam, peeled and diced into cubes
I½ tablespoons (30 g) pure maple syrup
½ tablespoon (8 ml) oil
¼ teaspoon cinnamon
⅛ teaspoon salt

FOR THE DOUGHNUTS:
½ cup (60 g) oat flour
½ cup (70 g) sweet rice flour
3 tablespoons (21 g) almond meal
2 tablespoons (26 g) pure cane sugar
I teaspoon cinnamon
I teaspoon baking powder
½ teaspoon salt
2 large eggs
¼ cup + 2 tablespoons (88 ml) milk
¼ cup (80 g) pure maple syrup
3 tablespoons (46 g) sweet potato purée
2 tablespoons (28 ml) oil
I tablespoon (15 g) unsweetened applesauce
2 teaspoons vanilla extract
¾ cup (102 g) diced roasted sweet potatoes

FOR THE TOPPING:
¾ cup (150 g) pure cane sugar
½ teaspoon cinnamon
2 tablespoons (40 g) pure maple syrup
4 tablespoons (55 g) butter, melted

TO MAKE THE ROASTED SWEET POTATOES: Preheat your oven to 400°F (200°C, or gas mark 6) and line a baking sheet with parchment paper. Toss the sweet potatoes with the rest of the ingredients to coat and spread in a single layer on the pan. Roast for 20 to 25 minutes, stirring once halfway through, until fork-tender and golden brown. Let fully cool.

TO MAKE THE DOUGHNUTS: Preheat your oven to 350°F (180°C, or gas mark 4) and grease your doughnut pan.

Mix the oat flour, sweet rice flour, almond meal, cane sugar, cinnamon, baking powder, and salt in a large bowl. In another bowl, whisk the eggs together. Then whisk in the milk, maple syrup, sweet potato purée, oil, applesauce, and vanilla extract.

Pour the wet mixture into the dry ingredients and stir with a large wooden spoon until just combined, being careful not to overmix. Gently fold in the sweet potatoes.

Spoon the batter into the doughnut molds, filling to just below the top of each mold, $1/8$- to ¼-inch (3 to 6 mm) from the top. Bake for 20 to 24 minutes until lightly golden brown around the edges. A toothpick inserted in the center should come out clean. Let cool in the pan for 5 minutes. Slide a thin spatula around the edges of the doughnuts to help loosen them out. Then place on a cooling rack and allow to cool fully before topping.

TO MAKE THE TOPPING: Preheat oven to broil, placing a rack at the top. Place an oven-safe wire rack on a rimmed baking sheet.

Mix the cane sugar and cinnamon in a bowl. In another bowl, whisk the maple syrup into the melted butter. Brush the dough-nuts on all sides with the butter and coat fully with the cinnamon-sugar mixture. Place each doughnut on the wire rack and then place under the broiler, watching closely, for I to 3 minutes until the sugar starts to bubble and melt. Gently flip over. Broil for another I to 3 minutes. Remove from the oven. As the doughnuts cool, they will firm and form a crunchy outer coating.

CHOCOLATE CINNAMON ROLL DOUGHNUTS
WITH MAPLE CREAM CHEESE ICING

yield: 10 to 12 standard doughnuts

The cinnamon roll is a pretty perfect thing. So, how would one go about making it even more irresistible? That's easy. Add chocolate and maple syrup and turn it into a handheld, portable doughnut. I believe the only thing left to do is start baking!

RECOMMENDED PANS:
Standard, mini, twist

FOR THE FILLING:
½ cup (115 g) packed brown sugar
½ teaspoon cinnamon
¼ cup (55 g) butter, melted

FOR THE DOUGHNUTS:
½ cup (60 g) oat flour
½ cup (70 g) sweet rice flour
¼ cup (20 g) unsweetened cocoa powder
3 tablespoons (21 g) almond meal
3 tablespoons cup (39 g) pure cane sugar
1 teaspoon cinnamon
1 teaspoon baking powder
½ teaspoon salt
2 large eggs
½ cup (120 ml) buttermilk
¼ cup (60 g) unsweetened applesauce
3 tablespoons (60 g) pure maple syrup
2 tablespoons (28 ml) oil
1½ teaspoons vanilla extract

FOR THE ICING:
¼ cup (60 g) cream cheese, softened
¾ cup (90 g) powdered sugar
2 tablespoons (40 g) pure maple syrup
½ teaspoon vanilla extract
¼ to ½ teaspoon cinnamon

TO MAKE THE FILLING: Stir the brown sugar and cinnamon into the melted butter with a fork until combined. Set aside.

TO MAKE THE DOUGHNUTS: Preheat your oven to 350°F (180°C, or gas mark 4) and grease your doughnut pan.

Combine the oat flour, sweet rice flour, cocoa powder, almond meal, cane sugar, cinnamon, baking powder, and salt in a large bowl, mixing well. In another bowl, whisk the eggs together. Then whisk in the buttermilk, applesauce, maple syrup, oil, and vanilla extract.

Pour the wet mixture into the dry ingredients and stir with a large wooden spoon until just combined, being careful not to overmix (stop when you no longer see dry flour).

Spoon 2 to 3 teaspoons (10 to 15 g) of the filling, evenly distributed, in each doughnut mold before adding the batter.

Spoon the batter into the doughnut molds, filling to just below the top of each mold, ⅛- to ¼-inch (3 to 6 mm) from the top. Bake for 18 to 22 minutes until lightly golden brown around the edges. A toothpick inserted in the center should come out clean. Let cool in the pan for 5 minutes. Slide a thin spatula around the edges of the doughnuts to help loosen them out. Then place on a cooling rack and allow to cool fully before icing.

TO MAKE THE ICING: Beat the cream cheese and powdered sugar together until fluffy and smooth. Beat in the maple syrup, vanilla extract, and cinnamon until creamy.

Scoop contents into a sealable plastic bag and cut a tiny hole in the corner. Pipe over the doughnuts in a zigzag pattern and serve.

KITCHEN SINK DOUGHNUTS
WITH EVERYTHING BUT THE KITCHEN SINK ON TOP

yield: 10 to 12 standard doughnuts

Do you ever have a hard time deciding on what flavors or toppings to add to doughnuts, muffins, cakes, and the like? Well, this will solve that problem and cure any and all sweets cravings you currently have: white chocolate, dark chocolate, banana, pecans, coconut, and more. Your mouth is about to do a giant happy dance with this one.

RECOMMENDED PANS:
Standard, holes, twist

FOR THE DOUGHNUTS:
½ cup (60 g) oat flour
½ cup (70 g) sweet rice flour
3 tablespoons (21 g) almond meal
2½ tablespoons (33 g) pure cane sugar
1 teaspoon baking powder
½ teaspoon salt
2 large eggs
⅓ cup (80 ml) milk
⅓ cup (75 g) well-mashed banana
3 tablespoons (45 g) unsweetened
    applesauce
3 tablespoons (60 g) pure maple syrup
2 tablespoons (28 ml) melted coconut oil
2 teaspoons vanilla extract
½ cup (40 g) unsweetened shredded
    coconut
½ cup (88 g) dark chocolate chips

FOR THE TOPPING:
½ cup (130 g) creamy peanut butter
½ cup (120 ml) milk
3 tablespoons (60 g) pure maple syrup
1 tablespoon (15 ml) coconut oil, melted
Chopped toasted pecans
Unsweetened shredded coconut
White chocolate shavings

FOR THE DRIZZLE:
¼ cup (44 g) dark chocolate chips
1 teaspoon unrefined coconut oil

TO MAKE THE DOUGHNUTS: Preheat your oven to 350°F (180°C, or gas mark 4) and grease your doughnut pan.

Combine the oat flour, sweet rice flour, almond meal, cane sugar, baking powder, and salt in a bowl, mixing well. In another bowl, whisk the eggs together. Then whisk in the milk, banana, apple-sauce, oil, maple syrup, and vanilla extract.

Pour the wet mixture into the dry ingredients and stir with a large wooden spoon until just combined, being careful not to overmix (stop when you no longer see dry flour). Gently fold in the coconut and chocolate chips.

Spoon the batter into the doughnut molds, filling to just below the top of each mold, ⅛- to ¼-inches (3 to 6 mm) from the top. Bake for 18 to 22 minutes until lightly golden brown around the edges. A toothpick inserted in the center should come out clean. Let cool in the pan for 5 minutes. Slide a thin spatula around the edges of the doughnuts to help loosen them out. Then place on a cooling rack and allow to cool fully before topping.

TO MAKE THE TOPPING: Whisk the peanut butter and milk together. It will start to break up and combine as you mix. Continue until the two are fully combined and creamy. Mix in the maple syrup and coconut oil until smooth.

Spread over the doughnuts and then top with pecans, coconut, and white chocolate shavings.

TO MAKE THE DRIZZLE: Melt the chocolate and coconut oil in a double boiler, stirring until smooth, or microwave for 30-second increments, stirring after each interval until smooth. Remove from heat, drizzle the chocolate over the doughnuts, and let set until the chocolate has hardened.

CHAPTER 7

savory specialties

WHO'S READY TO BE MADE A CONVERT?

• •

While you may have a little skepticism thinking about savory doughnuts, I urge you to dive right in. Once you start, you'll understand my obsession and need to create an entire chapter with savory options. Plus, I know many of you are on the lookout for sugar-free options, which you'll find plenty of here. This chapter will have you completely rethinking the idea of the doughnut. They're not just for breakfast and dessert any more!

• •

GARLIC CHEDDAR HERB DOUGHNUTS
WITH SHARP CHEDDAR CHEESE STUFFED INSIDE

● ● ● ● ● ● ● ● ● ● ● ● ● ● ● *yield: 6 to 8 standard doughnuts* ● ● ● ● ● ● ● ● ● ● ● ● ● ● ●

This cheese-and-herb laced doughnut will be your new favorite substitute for dinner rolls. Although, you may have to hide them so they actually make it to the table. The fresh herb flavor and melted sharp Cheddar cheese are irresistible!

RECOMMENDED PANS:
Standard, twist

FOR THE DOUGHNUTS:
½ cup (60 g) oat flour
½ cup (70 g) sweet rice flour
3 tablespoons (21 g) almond meal
I teaspoon baking powder
¾ teaspoon salt
½ teaspoon black pepper
½ teaspoon garlic granules
2 large eggs
6 tablespoons (90 ml) buttermilk
3 tablespoons (45 ml) oil
¼ cup (60 g) unsweetened applesauce
¾ cup (90 g) grated sharp Cheddar
  cheese
3 tablespoons (12 g) finely chopped
  parsley
2 tablespoons (12 g) diced scallions
I tablespoon (4 g) finely chopped
  oregano

FOR THE TOPPING (OPTIONAL):
Butter
Cream cheese

Preheat your oven to 350°F (180°C, or gas mark 4) and grease your doughnut pan.

Combine the oat flour, sweet rice flour, almond meal, baking powder, salt, black pepper, and garlic granules in a large bowl, mixing well. In another bowl, whisk the eggs together. Then whisk in the buttermilk, oil, and applesauce.

Pour the wet mixture into the dry ingredients and stir with a large wooden spoon until just combined, being careful not to overmix (stop when you no longer see dry flour). Gently fold in the cheese, parsley, scallions, and oregano.

Spoon the batter into the doughnut molds, filling to just below the top of each mold, $1/8$- to ¼-inch (3 to 6 mm) from the top. Bake for 18 to 22 minutes until lightly golden brown around the edges. A toothpick inserted in the center should come out clean. Let cool in the pan for 5 minutes. Slide a thin spatula around the edges of the doughnuts to help loosen them out. Then place on a cooling rack and allow to cool. Top with butter or cream cheese if desired.

VEGAN GARLIC SPINACH DOUGHNUTS
WITH BASIL CREAM SAUCE AND CRUNCHY PEPITAS

yield: 6 to 8 standard doughnuts

Savory flavors fill this doughnut from top to bottom and finish with a crunchy pepita bite!

RECOMMENDED PANS:
Standard, twist

FOR THE DOUGHNUTS:
½ cup (60 g) oat flour
½ cup (70 g) sweet rice flour
3 tablespoons (21 g) almond meal
3 tablespoons (18 g) nutritional yeast
2 tablespoons (14 g) ground flax meal
I teaspoon baking powder
½ teaspoon baking soda
½ teaspoon salt
½ teaspoon black pepper
¼ teaspoon garlic powder
¼ teaspoon onion granules
½ cup (120 ml) unsweetened almond milk
3 tablespoons (45 ml) oil
¼ cup (60 g) unsweetened applesauce
½ cup (15 g) finely chopped baby spinach

FOR THE SAUCE:
I cup (230 g) cashew cream (page 128)
½ cup (20 g) loosely packed chopped basil
¼ cup (24 g) nutritional yeast
½ teaspoon black pepper
¼ teaspoon garlic powder
¼ to ½ teaspoon salt
I to 2 tablespoons (15 to 28 ml) unsweetened almond milk

FOR THE TOPPING:
Pepitas
Large flaked sea salt

TO MAKE THE DOUGHNUTS: Preheat your oven to 350°F (180°C, or gas mark 4) and grease your doughnut pan.

Combine the oat flour, sweet rice flour, almond meal, nutritional yeast, ground flax, baking powder, baking soda, salt, black pepper, garlic powder, and onion granules in a large bowl, mixing well. In another bowl, whisk the milk, oil, and applesauce.

Pour the wet mixture into the dry ingredients and stir with a large wooden spoon until just combined, being careful not to overmix (stop when you no longer see dry flour). Gently fold in the spinach. Let sit for 5 minutes. The mixture will be very thick.

Spoon the mixture into a sealable plastic bag and cut a small tip off the end (about ¼ inch [6 mm] diagonal cut) and seal. Slowly squeeze the mixture into each doughnut mold, working your way around, until the molds are about ¼ inch (6 mm) from the top of the pan. Lightly spread with a small silicone spatula if needed. Bake for 20 to 24 minutes until lightly golden brown around the edges. A toothpick inserted in the center should come out clean. Let cool in the pan for 10 minutes.

Gently slide a thin spatula around the edges of the doughnuts to help loosen them out. Then place on a cooling rack and allow to cool fully before topping. The doughnuts will be slightly fragile while warm.

TO MAKE THE SAUCE: Place the cashew cream (page 128) in your high-speed blender with the basil, nutritional yeast, pepper, garlic powder, and salt. Start on medium speed and work up to high until you reach a fully smooth consistency. Add I tablespoon (15 ml) of milk at a time if needed to thin out. You want a thick, spreadable (not runny) sauce. Scrape the sides as needed. Taste and add more salt or pepper if desired. Remove from the blender and chill.

Spread over the doughnut and top with pepitas and a sprinkle of sea salt. Store the excess cashew sauce in an airtight container in the refrigerator for up to 4 days.

CORNBREAD DOUGHNUTS
WITH LIGHTLY SWEETENED HONEY BUTTER

yield: 8 to 10 standard doughnuts

I have always been a huge fan of cornbread. Whether it's breakfast, lunch, or dinner, cornbread is appropriate at any time of the day. In this recipe, traditional cornbread takes on a lighter doughnut texture while still holding that comforting cornbread flavor I adore so much.

RECOMMENDED PANS:
Standard, mini, holes, twist

FOR THE DOUGHNUTS:
⅓ cup (40 g) oat flour
⅓ cup (47 g) fine grain cornmeal
⅓ cup (39 g) masa harina
3 tablespoons (26 g) sweet rice flour
2 tablespoons (14 g) almond meal
2 teaspoons baking powder
¾ teaspoon salt
2 large eggs
½ cup (120 ml) milk
3 tablespoons (45 g) unsweetened
  applesauce
2 tablespoons (40 g) honey
2 tablespoons (28 g) butter, melted and
  slightly cooled

FOR THE HONEY BUTTER:
½ cup (112 g) unsalted butter, softened
2½ tablespoons (50 g) honey
¼ teaspoon salt

TO MAKE THE DOUGHNUTS: Preheat your oven to 350°F (180°C, or gas mark 4) and grease your doughnut pan.

Combine the oat flour, cornmeal, masa harina, sweet rice flour, almond meal, baking powder, and salt in a large bowl, mixing well. In another bowl, whisk the eggs together. Then whisk in the milk, applesauce, honey, and butter.

Pour the wet mixture into the dry ingredients and stir with a large wooden spoon until just combined, being careful not to overmix (stop when you no longer see dry flour). Let the batter sit for 5 minutes. The mixture will be thick.

Spoon the batter into the doughnut molds, filling to just below the top of each mold, ⅛- to ¼-inch (3 to 6 mm) from the top. Bake for 18 to 22 minutes until lightly golden brown around the edges. A toothpick inserted in the center should come out clean. Let cool in the pan for 5 minutes. Slide a thin spatula around the edges of the doughnuts to help loosen them out. Then place on a cooling rack for another 5 minutes. They are best served warm.

TO MAKE THE HONEY BUTTER: Mix the honey butter ingredients together until smooth. Spread on top of the doughnuts and store the excess in the fridge in a sealed container.

JALAPEÑO CHEDDAR DOUGHNUTS
WITH CREAMY CHEDDAR CHEESE SAUCE

yield: 8 to 10 standard doughnuts

This doughnut is for people who enjoy a little savory spice in their lives. It's stuffed with jalapeños and finished with a thick and creamy cheddar cheese sauce. Spread it on as a topping or just dunk your doughnut right in.

RECOMMENDED PANS:
Standard, twist

FOR THE DOUGHNUTS:
½ cup (60 g) oat flour
½ cup (70 g) sweet rice flour
¼ cup (30 g) grated sharp Cheddar cheese
3 tablespoons (21 g) almond meal
1 teaspoon baking powder
¾ teaspoon salt
¼ teaspoon black pepper
⅛ teaspoon garlic powder
2 large eggs
¼ cup + 2 tablespoons (88 ml) milk
¼ cup (60 g) unsweetened applesauce
3 tablespoons (45 ml) oil
¼ cup (34 g) diced pickled jalapeño peppers

FOR THE SAUCE:
½ cup (120 ml) milk
1 tablespoon (14 g) butter
1 tablespoon (9 g) sweet rice flour
¼ teaspoon black pepper
⅛ teaspoon salt
1/16 teaspoon garlic powder
¾ cup (90 g) grated sharp Cheddar cheese

FOR THE TOPPING:
Diced pickled jalapeños

TO MAKE THE DOUGHNUTS: Preheat your oven to 350°F (180°C, or gas mark 4) and grease your doughnut pan.

Combine the oat flour, sweet rice flour, Cheddar cheese, almond meal, baking powder, salt, black pepper, and garlic powder in a large bowl, mixing well. In another bowl, whisk the eggs together. Then whisk in the milk, applesauce, and oil.

Pour the wet mixture into the dry ingredients and stir with a large wooden spoon until just combined, being careful not to overmix (stop when you no longer see dry flour). Gently fold in the jalapeños.

Spoon the batter into the doughnut molds, filling to just below the top of each mold, ⅛- to ¼-inch (3 to 6 mm) from the top. Bake for 18 to 22 minutes until lightly golden brown around the edges. A toothpick inserted in the center should come out clean. Let cool in the pan for 5 minutes. Slide a thin spatula around the edges of the doughnuts to help loosen them out. Then place on a cooling rack and allow to cool fully before topping.

TO MAKE THE SAUCE: In a saucepan over medium heat, combine 2 tablespoons (28 ml) milk, butter, and flour and whisk until a paste forms. Add the rest of the milk and whisk until combined. Heat to boil, stirring frequently, and then reduce heat to low and simmer until thickened, stirring constantly, for 1 to 2 minutes. Remove from heat and stir in seasonings and cheese until melted. Spoon over the doughnuts or serve as a dip. Top with jalapeños, if desired.

ASIAGO CHEESE DOUGHNUTS
WITH BROILED ASIAGO CHEESE

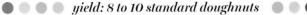 *yield: 8 to 10 standard doughnuts*

The salty and sharp flavor of Asiago cheese is not only melted inside but also broiled lightly on top of this seasoned doughnut. Just when you thought you missed eating bagels, this doughnut came in to save the day.

RECOMMENDED PANS:
Standard, twist

FOR THE DOUGHNUTS:
½ cup (60 g) oat flour
½ cup (70 g) sweet rice flour
¼ cup (25 g) grated Asiago cheese
3 tablespoons (21 g) almond meal
1 teaspoon baking powder
½ teaspoon salt
½ teaspoon oregano
¼ + ⅛ teaspoon garlic powder
2 large eggs
¼ cup + 3 tablespoons (105 ml) buttermilk
¼ cup (60 g) unsweetened applesauce
3 tablespoons (42 g) butter, melted and slightly cooled

FOR THE TOPPING:
4 tablespoons (55 g) butter, melted
¾ cup (75 g) grated Asiago cheese

TO MAKE THE DOUGHNUTS: Preheat your oven to 350°F (180°C, or gas mark 4) and grease your doughnut pan.

Combine the oat flour, sweet rice flour, Asiago cheese, almond meal, baking powder, salt, oregano, and garlic powder in a large bowl, mixing well. In another bowl, whisk the eggs together. Then whisk in the buttermilk, applesauce, and butter.

Pour the wet mixture into the dry ingredients and stir with a large wooden spoon until just combined, being careful not to overmix (stop when you no longer see dry flour).

Spoon the batter into the doughnut molds, filling to just below the top of each mold, ⅛- to ¼-inch (3 to 6 mm) from the top. Bake for 18 to 22 minutes until lightly golden brown around the edges. A toothpick inserted in the center should come out clean. Let cool in the pan for 5 minutes. Slide a thin spatula around the edges of the doughnuts to help loosen them out. Then place on a cooling rack and allow to cool fully before topping.

TO MAKE THE TOPPING: Preheat your oven to broil and place a rack in the top position.

Brush doughnuts lightly with butter and top with grated Asiago cheese. Place under the broiler for 1 to 3 minutes until the cheese is melted and just starts to brown. Remove from the oven and let cool for at least 10 to 15 minutes on the pan. The doughnuts will be fragile while hot but firm when cooled.

EVERYTHING DOUGHNUTS
WITH SIMPLE CREAM CHEESE SCHMEAR

yield: 6 to 8 standard doughnuts

Oh my gosh. This doughnut. Can I beg you to make it? Or can I come over and make it for you? Would that be weird? You won't care once it comes out of the oven. Trust me! It's just like an everything bagel but with a fluffy, soft doughnut chew. Get ready for some savory love.

RECOMMENDED PANS:
Standard, mini, holes, twist

FOR THE DOUGHNUTS:
½ cup (60 g) oat flour
½ cup (70 g) sweet rice flour
3 tablespoons (21 g) almond meal
1 teaspoon baking powder
½ teaspoon salt
2 large eggs
¼ cup + 2 tablespoons (88 ml) buttermilk
3 tablespoons (45 ml) oil
3 tablespoons (45 g) unsweetened applesauce

FOR THE TOPPING:
4 teaspoons (12 g) poppy seeds
4 teaspoons (11 g) sesame seeds
3 teaspoons (5 g) dried minced garlic
3 teaspoons (5 g) dried minced onion
1½ teaspoons flaked sea salt
4 tablespoons (55 g) butter, melted
Cream cheese, to top

TO MAKE THE DOUGHNUTS: Preheat your oven to 350°F (180°C, or gas mark 4) and grease your doughnut pan.

Combine the oat flour, sweet rice flour, almond meal, baking powder, and salt in a large bowl, mixing well. In another bowl, whisk the eggs together. Then whisk in the buttermilk, oil, and applesauce.

Pour the wet mixture into the dry ingredients and stir with a large wooden spoon until just combined, being careful not to overmix (stop when you no longer see dry flour).

Spoon the batter into the doughnut molds, filling to just below the top of each mold, ⅛- to ¼-inch (3 to 6 mm) from the top. Bake for 18 to 22 minutes until lightly golden brown around the edges. A toothpick inserted in the center should come out clean. Let cool in the pan for 5 minutes. Slide a thin spatula around the edges of the doughnuts to help loosen them out. Then place on a cooling rack and allow to cool fully before topping.

TO MAKE THE TOPPING: Preheat your oven to 375°F (190°C, or gas mark 5) and place an oven-safe wire rack on a baking sheet.

Mix the poppy seeds, sesame seeds, dried garlic, dried onion, and salt together in a bowl. Brush the top of each doughnut with the melted butter and then invert the doughnut into the seed mixture. Sprinkle with extra poppy seeds if desired. Place each doughnut on the wire rack and then bake for 5 minutes. Remove from the oven and let cool. The doughnuts will be fragile while hot but firm when cooled. Serve with cream cheese.

FRENCH ONION DOUGHNUTS
WITH BROILED GRUYÈRE CHEESE

● ● ● ● ● ● ● ● ● ● ● ● ● ● ● ● *yield: 8 to 10 standard doughnuts* ● ● ● ● ● ● ● ● ● ● ● ● ●

This savory treat is stuffed with French onion soup flavor. Just as the classic soup is topped with Gruyère cheese, you'll finish these doughnuts in the same way. Dunk in a hot bowl of soup or eat all on its own. Either way works!

RECOMMENDED PANS:
Standard, holes

FOR THE ONIONS:
I tablespoon (15 ml) extra-virgin olive oil
I medium yellow onion, diced

FOR THE DOUGHNUTS:
½ cup (60 g) oat flour
½ cup (70 g) sweet rice flour
3 tablespoons (21 g) almond meal
I teaspoon baking powder
½ teaspoon dried basil
½ teaspoon garlic powder
½ teaspoon dried thyme
½ teaspoon black pepper
½ teaspoon salt
2 large eggs
⅓ cup (80 ml) mushroom broth
3 tablespoons (45 g) unsweetened
   applesauce
3 tablespoons (45 ml) extra-virgin
   olive oil
½ cup (44 g) cooked onions

FOR THE TOPPING:
6 ounces (170 g) Gruyère or Jarlsberg
   cheese, grated
Black pepper

TO MAKE THE ONIONS: Heat the oil in a small pan over medium-low heat. Once hot, add in the diced onion and cook for 8 to 10 minutes until softened. Remove from heat and let cool.

TO MAKE THE DOUGHNUTS: Preheat your oven to 350°F (180°C, or gas mark 4) and grease your doughnut pan.

Combine the oat flour, sweet rice flour, almond meal, baking powder, basil, garlic powder, thyme, black pepper, and salt in a large bowl, mixing well. In another bowl, whisk the eggs together. Then whisk in the mushroom broth, applesauce, and oil.

Pour the wet mixture into the dry ingredients and stir with a large wooden spoon until just combined, being careful not to overmix (stop when you no longer see dry flour). Gently fold in the cooked onions.

Spoon the batter into the doughnut molds, filling to just below the top of each mold, $\frac{1}{8}$- to ¼-inch (3 to 6 mm) from the top. Bake for 18 to 22 minutes until lightly golden brown around the edges. A toothpick inserted in the center should come out clean. Let cool in the pan for 5 minutes. Slide a thin spatula around the edges of the doughnuts to help loosen them out. Then place on a cooling rack and allow to cool fully before topping.

TO MAKE THE TOPPING: Preheat your oven to broil and place a rack in the top position.

Place doughnuts on a baking sheet and top with grated cheese. Broil for I to 3 minutes, watching closely, until the cheese is melted and bubbly. Remove from the oven and top with a sprinkle of black pepper. Serve warm.

BASIL GARLIC DOUGHNUTS
WITH SUNDRIED TOMATO CREAM CHEESE SPREAD AND PINE NUTS

yield: 6 to 8 standard doughnuts

This will most definitely remind you of eating a bagel smothered in sundried tomato cream cheese. Except for the fact that the fluffy, light doughnut texture will make things even tastier. Top this savory creation with basil and toasted pine nuts and you'll never want another bagel again.

RECOMMENDED PANS:
Standard, mini, holes, twist

FOR THE DOUGHNUTS:
½ cup (60 g) oat flour
½ cup (70 g) sweet rice flour
3 tablespoons (21 g) almond meal
1 teaspoon baking powder
¾ teaspoon salt
½ teaspoon garlic powder
¼ teaspoon black pepper
2 large eggs
⅓ cup (80 ml) milk
¼ cup (60 g) unsweetened applesauce
2 tablespoons (28 ml) oil
2½ tablespoons (6 g) finely chopped basil

FOR THE SPREAD:
½ cup (115 g) cream cheese, softened
½ tablespoon olive oil
¼ teaspoon salt
⅛ teaspoon black pepper
¼ cup (28 g) diced oil-packed sundried tomatoes

FOR THE TOPPING:
Chopped basil
Toasted pine nuts

TO MAKE THE DOUGHNUTS: Preheat your oven to 350°F (180°C, or gas mark 4) and grease your doughnut pan.

Combine the oat flour, sweet rice flour, almond meal, baking powder, salt, garlic powder, and black pepper in a large bowl, mixing well. In another bowl, whisk the eggs together. Then whisk in the milk, applesauce, and oil.

Pour the wet mixture into the dry ingredients and stir with a large wooden spoon until just combined, being careful not to overmix (stop when you no longer see dry flour). Gently fold in the basil.

Spoon the batter into the doughnut molds, filling to just below the top of each mold, ⅛- to ¼-inch (3 to 6 mm) from the top. Bake for 18 to 22 minutes until lightly golden brown around the edges. A toothpick inserted in the center should come out clean. Let cool in the pan for 5 minutes. Slide a thin spatula around the edges of the doughnuts to help loosen them out. Then place on a cooling rack and allow to cool fully before topping.

TO MAKE THE SPREAD: Combine the cream cheese, olive oil, salt, and black pepper and mix with a fork until creamy. Blot the sundried tomatoes with a paper towel to soak up the extra oil and then stir into the cream cheese mixture until evenly distributed. Spread onto the doughnuts and top with chopped basil and toasted pine nuts.

VEGAN GREEN CHILE DOUGHNUTS
WITH NACHO CASHEW CREAM SAUCE

yield: 8 to 10 standard doughnuts

Green chiles and spiced flavors emanate through every bite of this doughnut. You could eat the doughnut alone, but you should definitely go through the trouble of making the nacho cashew cream sauce. If
you can actually get the sauce on top before eating it all with tortilla chips, I will be impressed.

RECOMMENDED PANS:
Standard, holes

FOR THE DOUGHNUTS:
½ cup (60 g) oat flour
⅓ cup (39 g) masa harina
¼ cup (35 g) sweet rice flour
2 tablespoons (14 g) almond meal
2 tablespoons (14 g) ground flax meal
I teaspoon baking powder
¾ teaspoon salt
½ teaspoon chili powder
¼ teaspoon garlic powder
¼ teaspoon cayenne pepper
¾ cup (175 ml) unsweetened almond milk
3 tablespoons (45 ml) oil
3 tablespoons (45 g) unsweetened
   applesauce
⅓ cup (40 g) canned diced green chiles

FOR THE CASHEW CREAM:
1¼ cups (175 g) raw cashews
¼ to ⅔ cup (60 to 160 ml) unsweetened
   almond milk

FOR THE NACHO SAUCE:
¼ cup (30 g) canned diced green chiles
¼ cup (38 g) diced red bell pepper
3 tablespoons (18 g) nutritional yeast
I teaspoon chili powder
½ teaspoon cumin
¼ teaspoon garlic powder
¼ to ½ teaspoon each salt and pepper
⅛ teaspoon cayenne pepper

TO MAKE THE DOUGHNUTS: Preheat your oven to 350°F (180°C,
or gas mark 4) and grease your doughnut pan.

Combine the oat flour, masa harina, sweet rice flour, almond
meal, ground flax meal, baking powder, salt, chili powder, garlic
powder, and cayenne pepper in a large bowl, mixing well. In
another bowl, whisk the milk, oil, and applesauce.

Pour the wet mixture into the dry ingredients and stir with a
large wooden spoon until just combined, being careful not to
overmix (stop when you no longer see dry flour). Gently fold
in the green chiles. Let the batter rest for 3 to 5 minutes. The
batter will be very thick.

Spoon the mixture into a sealable plastic bag and cut a small tip
off the end (about ¼ inch [6 mm] diagonal cut) and seal. Slowly
squeeze the mixture into each doughnut mold, working your way
around and until the molds are about ¼ inch (6 mm) from the top
of the pan. Try to squeeze an even layer, only going around the
mold once if possible. Lightly spread with a spatula if needed.

Bake for 20 to 24 minutes until lightly golden brown around the
edges. A toothpick inserted in the center should come out clean.
Let cool in the pan for 10 minutes.

Gently slide a thin spatula around the edges of the doughnuts
to help loosen them out. Then place on a cooling rack and allow
to cool fully before topping. The doughnuts will be slightly fragile
while warm.

TO MAKE THE CASHEW CREAM: Soak cashews in water for at least
4 hours or overnight. Drain and rinse the cashews.

Place the cashews in your high-speed blender, starting with ¼
cup (60 ml) milk. Scrape the sides as necessary to keep things
moving. Add milk slowly until you reach a creamy, smooth, and
thick consistency. Use the least amount of milk as possible.

TO MAKE THE NACHO SAUCE: Scrape out the cashew cream mixture from the blender. Measure I cup (230 g) of cashew cream and place it back in the blender with the other nacho sauce ingredients. Start on medium speed and work up to high until you reach a fully smooth consistency, adding more almond milk if needed to thin out. Scrape the sides as needed. Taste and add more salt or pepper if desired. Remove from the blender and chill.

Place the sauce in a small plastic bag, seal the bag, and cut a tiny tip from the bottom corner (about $\frac{1}{8}$ inch [3 mm] long). Squeeze the sauce over the doughnut or place in a bowl to use as a dip or spread.

Store the excess in a sealed container in the refrigerator for up to 4 days.

GREEK STUFFED DOUGHNUTS
WITH FETA CREAM CHEESE SPREAD

yield: 8 to 10 standard doughnuts

Spinach, olives, and sundried tomatoes run throughout the inside of this doughnut, making each and every bite a little savory treasure. It's topped with a feta cream cheese spread that is going to become a new favorite. You will soon be looking for any excuse to use it—on eggs, on toast, on vegetables? Whatever suits your fancy, but most definitely use it on this doughnut.

RECOMMENDED PANS:
Standard, holes, twist

FOR THE COOKED ONION:
I small red onion, diced
½ tablespoon extra-virgin olive oil

FOR THE DOUGHNUTS:
½ cup (60 g) oat flour
½ cup (70 g) sweet rice flour
3 tablespoons (21 g) almond meal
1½ teaspoons dried oregano
I teaspoon baking powder
¾ teaspoon salt
½ teaspoon black pepper
¼ teaspoon garlic powder
2 large eggs
⅓ cup (80 ml) milk
¼ cup (60 g) unsweetened applesauce
3 tablespoons (45 ml) extra-virgin
   olive oil
⅓ cup (10 g) finely chopped baby
   spinach
¼ cup (28 g) oil-packed sundried
   tomatoes, chopped and blotted
3 tablespoons (17 g) cooked red onion
3 tablespoons (25 g) pitted and diced
   kalamata olives

FOR THE SPREAD:
I cup (150 g) crumbled feta, softened
⅓ cup (77 g) cream cheese, softened
2 to 4 tablespoons (28 to 60 ml) milk
Cracked black pepper to top

TO MAKE THE ONIONS: Heat the oil in a small pan over medium-low heat. Once hot, add in the diced onion and cook for 8 to 10 minutes until softened, stirring frequently. Remove from heat and let cool.

TO MAKE THE DOUGHNUTS: Preheat your oven to 350°F (180°C, or gas mark 4) and grease your doughnut pan.

Combine the oat flour, sweet rice flour, almond meal, oregano, baking powder, salt, black pepper, and garlic powder in a large bowl, mixing well. In another bowl, whisk the eggs together. Then whisk in the milk, applesauce, and oil.

Pour the wet mixture into the dry ingredients and stir with a large wooden spoon until just combined, being careful not to overmix (stop when you no longer see dry flour). Gently fold in the spinach, tomatoes, onion, and olives.

Spoon the batter into the doughnut molds, filling to just below the top of each mold, ⅛- to ¼-inch (3 to 6 mm) from the top. Bake for 18 to 22 minutes until lightly golden brown around the edges. A toothpick inserted in the center should come out clean. Let cool in the pan for 5 minutes. Slide a thin spatula around the edges of the doughnuts to help loosen them. Then place on a cooling rack and allow to cool fully before topping.

TO MAKE THE SPREAD: Beat the feta and cream cheese together until combined. Beat in the milk, starting with 2 tablespoons (28 ml) and adding more as needed. You are looking for a creamy but thick spread.

Spread on the doughnuts and top with cracked black pepper.

CHAPTER 8

healthed-up hits

DOUGHNUTS ON THE LIGHTER SIDE.

· ·

What you'll find here are a group of recipes that walk on the lighter side of the doughnut spectrum. But what you'll also find are doughnuts that are not lacking in flavor, texture, or creativity. I've brought a few extra ingredients to the table in this chapter that really set these doughnuts apart.

· ·

CHERRY VANILLA DOUGHNUTS
WITH HONEY-SWEETENED VANILLA YOGURT DIP

yield: 8 to 10 standard doughnuts

Vanilla meets cherry in this lightly honey-sweetened doughnut. In lieu of frosting, you'll combine Greek yogurt, vanilla beans, and honey to create an addictive doughnut dip. Any leftovers can be—and should be—eaten with a spoon.

RECOMMENDED PANS:
Standard, mini, holes, twist

FOR THE DOUGHNUTS:
½ cup (60 g) oat flour
½ cup (56 g) almond meal
¼ cup (35 g) sweet rice flour
2 tablespoons (14 g) ground flax meal
1 teaspoon baking powder
½ teaspoon salt
1 large egg
⅓ cup (80 ml) milk
¼ cup (80 g) honey
¼ cup (60 g) unsweetened applesauce
1 tablespoon (15 ml) oil
2 teaspoons vanilla bean paste
6 tablespoons (54 g) chopped dried cherries

FOR THE DIP:
1 cup (200 g) plain Greek yogurt
2 to 3 tablespoons (40 to 60 g) clover honey
1½ teaspoons vanilla bean paste

FOR THE TOPPING:
Dried cherries

TO MAKE THE DOUGHNUTS: Preheat your oven to 350°F (180°C, or gas mark 4) and grease your doughnut pan.

Combine the oat flour, almond meal, sweet rice flour, ground flax meal, baking powder, and salt in a large bowl, mixing well. In another bowl, whisk the egg. Then whisk in the milk, honey, applesauce, oil, and vanilla bean paste.

Pour the wet mixture into the dry ingredients and stir with a large wooden spoon until just combined, being careful not to overmix (stop when you no longer see dry flour). Gently fold in the chopped dried cherries.

Spoon the batter into the doughnut molds, filling to just below the top of each mold, ⅛- to ¼-inch (3 to 6 mm) from the top. Bake for 18 to 22 minutes until lightly golden brown around the edges. A toothpick inserted in the center should come out clean. Let cool in the pan for 5 minutes. Slide a thin spatula around the edges of the doughnuts to help loosen them out. Then place on a cooling rack and allow to cool fully before icing.

TO MAKE THE DIP: Whisk the dip ingredients together until fully combined. Serve as a dip for the doughnuts. Top with dried cherries, if desired.

CHOCOLATE MINT DOUGHNUTS
WITH CREAMY AVOCADO MINT FROSTING

yield: 8 to 10 standard doughnuts

The combination of chocolate and mint is classic. In this healthed-up version you have a chocolate-filled, honey-sweetened doughnut, with a nice kick of mint. The frosting is rich and creamy and actually made from avocado then infused with cocoa and mint for the perfect topping.

RECOMMENDED PANS:
Standard, mini, holes, twist

FOR THE DOUGHNUTS:
½ cup (60 g) oat flour
½ cup (56 g) almond meal
¼ cup (35 g) sweet rice flour
¼ cup (20 g) unsweetened cocoa
  powder
1½ tablespoons (11 g) ground flax meal
1 teaspoon baking powder
½ teaspoon salt
1 large egg
½ cup (120 ml) milk
¼ cup + 2 tablespoons (120 g) honey
¼ cup (60 g) unsweetened applesauce
1 tablespoon (15 ml) oil
1 teaspoon vanilla extract
¼ teaspoon peppermint extract

FOR THE FROSTING:
2 ripe avocados
5 to 8 tablespoons (100 to 160 g) clover
  honey or agave nectar
¼ to ½ teaspoon peppermint extract
Cocoa powder (optional), for topping

TO MAKE THE DOUGHNUTS: Preheat your oven to 350°F (180°C, or gas mark 4) and grease your doughnut pan.

Combine the oat flour, almond meal, sweet rice flour, cocoa powder, ground flax meal, baking powder, and salt in a large bowl, mixing well. In another bowl, whisk the egg. Then whisk in the milk, honey, applesauce, oil, vanilla extract, and peppermint extract.

Pour the wet mixture into the dry ingredients and stir with a large wooden spoon until just combined, being careful not to overmix (stop when you no longer see dry flour).

Spoon the batter into the doughnut molds, filling to just below the top of each mold, $1/8$- to ¼-inch (3 to 6 mm) from the top. Bake for 18 to 22 minutes until lightly golden brown around the edges. A toothpick inserted in the center should come out clean. Let cool in the pan for 5 minutes. Slide a thin spatula around the edges of the doughnuts to help loosen them out. Then place on a cooling rack and allow to cool fully before icing.

TO MAKE THE FROSTING: Process all the frosting ingredients except the cocoa in a food processor until creamy. Add more honey and/or peppermint extract if desired. Spread over the doughnuts and serve immediately. Dust with cocoa powder, if desired.

RECIPE NOTE

For a mint chocolate frosting, simply add ¼ cup (20 g) unsweetened cocoa powder to the food processor.

BANANA CORNBREAD DOUGHNUTS
WITH SIMPLE HONEY DRIZZLE

The flavor combination of this doughnut will totally surprise you. The banana adds sweetness and flavor to the recipe, while the masa harina and cornmeal bring that classic corn taste and texture you've always loved. These are a definite favorite in my house!

RECOMMENDED PANS:
Standard, twist

FOR THE DOUGHNUTS:
⅓ cup (39 g) masa harina
¼ cup (35 g) fine-ground cornmeal
¼ cup (30 g) oat flour
¼ cup (35 g) sweet rice flour
3 tablespoons (21 g) almond meal
2 tablespoons (14 g) ground flax meal
2 teaspoons baking powder
½ teaspoon salt
1 large egg
½ cup + 2 tablespoons (148 ml) milk
⅓ cup (75 g) mashed banana
3 tablespoons (60 g) honey
1 tablespoon (15 ml) oil
1 teaspoon vanilla extract

FOR THE TOPPING:
Honey

Preheat your oven to 350°F (180°C, or gas mark 4) and grease your doughnut pan.

Combine the masa harina, cornmeal, oat flour, sweet rice flour, almond meal, flax meal, baking powder, and salt in a large bowl, mixing well. In another bowl, whisk the egg. Then whisk in the milk, mashed banana, honey, oil, and vanilla extract.

Pour the wet mixture into the dry ingredients and stir with a large wooden spoon until just combined, being careful not to overmix (stop when you no longer see dry flour). Let the batter sit for 5 minutes to thicken.

Spoon the batter into the doughnut molds, filling to just below the top of each mold, ⅛- to ¼-inch (3 to 6 mm) from the top. Bake for 18 to 22 minutes until lightly golden brown around the edges. A toothpick inserted in the center should come out clean. Let cool in the pan for 5 minutes. Slide a thin spatula around the edges of the doughnuts to help loosen them out. Then place on a cooling rack and let cool for 5 to 10 minutes.

Top with a drizzle of honey and serve warm.

BLUEBERRY DOUGHNUTS
WITH HONEY-SWEETENED ALMOND BUTTER AND BANANAS

yield: 6 to 8 standard doughnuts

Blueberries, bananas, and almond butter are three foods that scream breakfast. Add a lightly sweetened, fluffy doughnut to the mix and you'll be ready to start your day.

RECOMMENDED PANS:
Standard, holes, twist

FOR THE DOUGHNUTS:
½ cup (60 g) oat flour
½ cup (56 g) almond meal
¼ cup (35 g) sweet rice flour
2 tablespoons (14 g) ground flax meal
1 teaspoon baking powder
½ teaspoon salt
1 large egg
⅓ cup (80 ml) milk
3 tablespoons (60 g) honey
¼ cup (60 g) unsweetened applesauce
1 tablespoon (15 ml) oil
2 teaspoons vanilla extract
½ cup (75 g) blueberries

FOR THE ALMOND BUTTER:
½ cup (130 g) creamy roasted almond butter
1 tablespoon (20 g) honey
1 tablespoon (14 g) unrefined coconut oil, melted

FOR THE TOPPING:
1 to 2 bananas, thinly sliced

TO MAKE THE DOUGHNUTS: Preheat your oven to 350°F (180°C, or gas mark 4) and grease your doughnut pan.

Combine the oat flour, almond meal, sweet rice flour, ground flax meal, baking powder, and salt in a large bowl, mixing well. In another bowl, whisk the egg. Then add in the milk, honey, applesauce, oil, and vanilla extract. Whisk until well combined.

Pour the wet mixture into the dry ingredients and stir with a large wooden spoon until just combined, being careful not to overmix (stop when you no longer see dry flour). Gently fold the blueberries into the batter.

Spoon the batter into the doughnut molds, filling to just below the top of each mold, ⅛- to ¼-inch (3 to 6 mm) from the top. Bake for 20 to 24 minutes until lightly golden brown around the edges. A toothpick inserted in the center should come out clean. Let cool in the pan for 5 minutes. Slide a thin spatula around the edges of the doughnuts to help loosen them out. Then place on a cooling rack and allow to cool fully before topping.

TO MAKE THE ALMOND BUTTER: Mix all of the ingredients together until smooth. Spread the topping over the doughnuts and then top with sliced banana and serve immediately.

TRIPLE BERRY DOUGHNUTS
WITH COCONUT BUTTER GLAZE

. . . . . yield: 6 to 8 standard doughnuts . . . .

During the summer months I am completely addicted to berries—all of them. I prefer to eat them raw, but once in a while I buy more berries than I can consume. This healthier doughnut utilizes those left-over berries and is topped with a naturally sweet coconut butter topping.

RECOMMENDED PANS:
Standard, holes

FOR THE DOUGHNUTS:
½ cup (60 g) oat flour
½ cup (50 g) almond meal
¼ cup (35 g) sweet rice flour
2 tablespoons (14 g) ground flax meal
1 teaspoon baking powder
½ teaspoon salt
1 large egg
¼ cup (60 ml) milk
3 tablespoons (60 g) honey
3 tablespoons (45 g) applesauce
1 tablespoon (15 ml) oil
1½ teaspoons vanilla extract
2 tablespoons (16 g) chopped
    raspberries
2 tablespoons (18 g) chopped
    blackberries
2 tablespoons (18 g) blueberries

FOR THE GLAZE:
¾ cup (168 g) coconut butter
1 tablespoon (14 g) unrefined coconut oil

FOR THE TOPPING:
Fresh blueberries, raspberries,
    and blackberries, halved
Honey (optional)

TO MAKE THE DOUGHNUTS: Preheat your oven to 350°F (180°C, or gas mark 4) and grease your doughnut pan.

Combine the oat flour, almond meal, sweet rice flour, ground flax meal, baking powder, and salt in a large bowl, mixing well. In another bowl, whisk the egg. Then whisk in the milk, honey, applesauce, oil, and vanilla extract.

Pour the wet mixture into the dry ingredients and stir with a large wooden spoon until just combined, being careful not to overmix (stop when you no longer see dry flour). Lightly blot the chopped berries with a paper towel, and then gently fold them into the batter.

Spoon the batter into the doughnut molds, filling to just below the top of each mold, ⅛- to ¼-inch (3 to 6 mm) from the top. Bake for 20 to 24 minutes until lightly golden brown around the edges. A toothpick inserted in the center should come out clean. Let cool in the pan for 5 minutes. Slide a thin spatula around the edges of the doughnuts to help loosen them out. Then place on a cooling rack and allow to cool fully before icing.

TO MAKE THE GLAZE: In a small saucepan over medium-low heat, gently melt the coconut butter and oil together, or melt in the microwave in 30-second increments, stirring after each interval, until smooth. Then stir in the honey until fully combined. Pour into a bowl and let cool on the counter for about 30 minutes.

Spread (or drizzle) the glaze over the doughnuts and then top with the halved fresh fruit. Let set until the glaze has hardened. Top with a drizzle of honey, if desired.

MAPLE CINNAMON DOUGHNUTS
WITH MAPLE CINNAMON ALMOND BUTTER GLAZE

yield: 8 to 10 standard doughnuts

Two of my all-time favorite flavors combine to create this healthed-up doughnut. A quick and easy maple cinnamon almond butter seals the deal for this magical, anytime treat.

RECOMMENDED PANS:
Standard, mini, holes

FOR THE DOUGHNUTS:
½ cup (60 g) oat flour
½ cup (56 g) almond meal
¼ cup (35 g) sweet rice flour
2 tablespoons (14 g) ground flax meal
1½ teaspoons cinnamon
1 teaspoon baking powder
½ teaspoon salt
1 large egg
⅓ cup (80 ml) milk
¼ cup (80 g) pure maple syrup
3 tablespoons (47 g) unsweetened
    applesauce
1 tablespoon (15 ml) oil
2 teaspoons vanilla extract

FOR THE GLAZE:
¾ cup (195 g) creamy roasted almond
    butter
3 tablespoons (42 g) unrefined coconut
    oil, melted
2 to 3 tablespoons (40 to 60 g) pure
    maple syrup, warmed
½ to ¾ teaspoon cinnamon
Sprinkles (optional)

TO MAKE THE DOUGHNUTS: Preheat your oven to 350°F (180°C, or gas mark 4) and grease your doughnut pan.

Combine the oat flour, almond meal, sweet rice flour, flax meal, cinnamon, baking powder, and salt in a large bowl, mixing well. In another bowl, whisk the egg. Then whisk in the milk, maple syrup, applesauce, oil, and vanilla extract.

Pour the wet mixture into the dry ingredients and stir with a large wooden spoon until just combined, being careful not to overmix (stop when you no longer see dry flour).

Spoon the batter into the doughnut molds, filling to just below the top of each mold, ⅛- to ¼-inch (3 to 6 mm) from the top. Bake for 18 to 22 minutes until lightly golden brown around the edges. A toothpick inserted in the center should come out clean. Let cool in the pan for 5 minutes. Slide a thin spatula around the edges of the doughnuts to help loosen them out. Then place on a cooling rack and allow to cool fully before topping.

TO MAKE THE GLAZE: Mix the almond butter and coconut oil together until smooth. Mix in the maple syrup and cinnamon until fully combined. Invert the doughnut into the glaze, letting the excess drip off, or drizzle glaze over doughnuts. Top with sprinkles, if desired.

GRAIN-FREE ORANGE ALMOND CHIA DOUGHNUTS
WITH COCONUT BUTTER OR HONEY TOPPING

yield: 8 to 10 standard doughnuts

This grain-free, orange- and almond-scented, chia-stuffed doughnut has a soft, incredibly moist texture that is definitely not lacking in flavor. It's one of my favorite breakfast doughnuts!

RECOMMENDED PANS:
Standard

FOR THE DOUGHNUTS:
1 cup (112 g) blanched almond flour
1 cup (112 g) almond meal
½ teaspoon baking soda
¼ teaspoon salt
2 large eggs
¼ cup (60 ml) no-sugar-added orange juice
¼ cup (60 ml) milk
3 tablespoons (42 g) unrefined coconut oil, melted and slightly cooled
¼ cup (80 g) honey
1 tablespoon (6 g) orange zest
1½ teaspoons vanilla extract
¼ teaspoon almond extract
2½ tablespoons (33 g) chia seeds

FOR THE TOPPING (OPTIONAL):
Melted coconut butter
Honey
Orange zest

TO MAKE THE DOUGHNUTS: Preheat your oven to 350°F (180°C, or gas mark 4) and grease your doughnut pan.

Combine the almond flour, almond meal, baking soda, and salt in a bowl, mixing well. In another bowl, whisk the eggs together. Then whisk in the orange juice, milk, oil, honey, orange zest, vanilla extract, and almond extract.

Pour the wet mixture into your blender and pour the dry ingredients on top. Start at low speed and work up to high until fully mixed and smooth, about 5 to 10 seconds. Scrape the sides if needed and blend again. Add the chia seeds and blend over medium-low speed until just incorporated.

Slowly pour the batter into the doughnut pan to just below the top of each mold, $1/8$- to ¼-inch (3 to 6 mm) from the top. Bake for 13 to 16 minutes until lightly golden brown around the edges. A toothpick inserted in the center should come out clean. Let cool in the pan for 5 minutes. Gently slide a thin spatula around the edges of the doughnuts to help loosen them out. Then place on a cooling rack and allow to cool fully before topping. Doughnuts will be fragile while warm but will firm as they cool.

TO MAKE THE TOPPING: These doughnuts are so moist and flavorful you don't even need a topping! However, feel free to add a drizzle of coconut butter or honey and a sprinkle of orange zest if desired.

GRAIN-FREE COCONUT CREAM DOUGHNUTS
WITH COCONUT CREAM HONEY GLAZE

yield: 8 to 10 standard doughnuts

This doughnut is grain-free and refined sugar–free but full of coconutty goodness inside and out. It's topped with a rich and thick coconut cream glaze that is totally acceptable to eat straight from the bowl. You're going to have a hard time keeping your hands off of these.

RECOMMENDED PANS:
Standard

FOR THE DOUGHNUTS:
1 cup + 2 tablespoons (126 g) blanched
   almond flour
2 tablespoons (14 g) coconut flour
1½ tablespoons (11 g) ground flax meal
½ teaspoon baking soda
¼ teaspoon salt
2 large eggs
¼ cup + 2 tablespoons (88 ml) milk
¼ cup (60 ml) honey
3 tablespoons (42 g) unrefined coconut
   oil, melted and slightly cooled
1½ teaspoons vanilla extract

FOR THE GLAZE:
¾ cup (180 g) coconut cream
2 tablespoons (28 g) unrefined coconut
   oil, melted and slightly cooled
2 tablespoons (40 g) clover honey
½ teaspoon vanilla bean paste

TO MAKE THE DOUGHNUTS: Preheat your oven to 350°F (180°C, or gas mark 4) and grease your doughnut pan.

Combine the almond flour, coconut flour, ground flax, baking soda, and salt in a bowl, mixing well. In another bowl, whisk the eggs together. Then whisk in the oil, milk, honey, and vanilla extract.

Pour the wet mixture into your blender and pour the dry ingredients on top. Start at low speed and work up to high until fully mixed and smooth, about 5 to 10 seconds. Scrape the sides if needed and blend again.

Slowly pour the batter into the doughnut pan to just below the top of each mold, ⅛- to ¼-inch (3 to 6 mm) from the top. Bake for 13 to 16 minutes until lightly golden brown around the edges. A toothpick inserted in the center should come out clean. Let cool in the pan for 5 minutes. Gently slide a thin spatula around the edges of the doughnuts to help loosen them out. Then place on a cooling rack and allow to cool fully before topping. The doughnuts will be fragile while warm but will firm as they cool.

TO MAKE THE GLAZE: Mix ingredients together until smooth. Invert the doughnuts into the topping, letting any excess drip off, or spread over each doughnut. Glaze will not fully set.

RECIPE NOTE

See page 10 for more details on coconut cream.

PUMPKIN SPICE COCONUT DOUGHNUTS
WITH PUMPKIN SPICE COCONUT CREAM GLAZE

yield: 10 to 12 standard doughnuts

Get ready for this lightened-up pumpkin doughnut that is not lacking in flavor, moisture, or texture. And as an added twist, I've added coconut inside and out.

RECOMMENDED PANS:
standard, mini, holes, twist

FOR THE DOUGHNUTS:
½ cup (60 g) oat flour
½ cup (56 g) almond meal
¼ cup (35 g) sweet rice flour
¼ cup (20 g) unsweetened shredded coconut
1½ tablespoons (11 g) ground flax meal
1 teaspoon baking powder
1 teaspoon cinnamon
½ teaspoon salt
½ teaspoon ground ginger
½ teaspoon ground nutmeg
¼ teaspoon ground allspice
⅛ teaspoon ground ground cloves
1 large egg
¼ cup + 2 tablespoons (88 ml) lite canned coconut milk
⅓ cup (82 g) pumpkin purée
¼ cup (80 g) honey
1½ tablespoons (23 g) unsweetened applesauce
1 tablespoon (14 g) unrefined coconut oil, melted and slightly cooled
2 teaspoons vanilla extract

FOR THE GLAZE:
½ cup (120 g) coconut cream
¼ cup (61 g) pumpkin purée
¼ cup (50 g) coconut sugar
½ teaspoon cinnamon
⅛ teaspoon ground ginger
Pinch ground nutmeg

FOR THE TOPPING:
Unsweetened flaked coconut

TO MAKE THE DOUGHNUTS: Preheat your oven to 350°F (180°C, or gas mark 4) and grease your doughnut pan.

Combine the oat flour, almond meal, sweet rice flour, coconut, flax meal, baking powder, cinnamon, salt, ginger, nutmeg, allspice, and ground cloves in a bowl, mixing well. In another bowl, whisk the egg. Then whisk in the milk, pumpkin purée, honey, applesauce, oil, and vanilla extract.

Pour the wet mixture into the dry ingredients and stir with a large wooden spoon until just combined, being careful not to overmix (stop when you no longer see dry flour).

Spoon the batter into the doughnut molds, filling to just below the top of each mold, ⅛- to ¼-inch (3 to 6 mm) from the top. Bake for 18 to 22 minutes until lightly golden brown around the edges. A toothpick inserted in the center should come out clean. Let cool in the pan for 5 minutes. Slide a thin spatula around the edges of the doughnuts to help loosen them out. Then place on a cooling rack and allow to fully cool before topping.

TO MAKE THE GLAZE: In a bowl, stir the coconut cream and pumpkin purée together until combined. Then stir in the coconut sugar, cinnamon, ginger, and nutmeg until smooth. Spread on the cooled doughnuts. Top with flaked coconut. The glaze will firm up as it sits.

RECIPE NOTE

Coconut sugar is an unrefined sugar that doesn't taste much like coconut at all. It has a deep caramel flavor and is found in the sap from the flower bud of the coconut tree. Unrefined sucanat can be substituted in its place.

PEANUT BUTTER AND JELLY DOUGHNUTS
WITH CREAMY PEANUT BUTTER

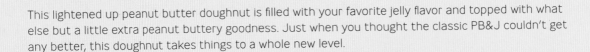

yield: 8 to 10 standard doughnuts

This lightened up peanut butter doughnut is filled with your favorite jelly flavor and topped with what else but a little extra peanut buttery goodness. Just when you thought the classic PB&J couldn't get any better, this doughnut takes things to a whole new level.

RECOMMENDED PANS:
Standard, holes, twist

FOR THE DOUGHNUTS:
½ cup (60 g) oat flour
¼ cup (28 g) almond meal
¼ cup (28 g) peanut meal
¼ cup (35 g) sweet rice flour
2 tablespoons (11 g) ground flax meal
1 teaspoon baking powder
½ teaspoon salt
1 large egg
6 tablespoons (60 ml) milk
¼ cup (60 g) unsweetened applesauce
¼ cup (65 g) peanut butter, melted
¼ cup (80 g) pure maple syrup
1 tablespoon (15 ml) oil
1½ teaspoons vanilla extract

FOR THE FILLING:
6 tablespoons (108 g) fruit-juice
   sweetened jelly

FOR THE TOPPING:
Creamy peanut butter

Preheat your oven to 350°F (180°C, or gas mark 4) and grease your doughnut pan.

Combine the oat flour, almond meal, peanut meal, sweet rice flour, flax meal, baking powder, and salt in a large bowl, mixing well. In another bowl, whisk the egg. Then whisk in the milk, applesauce, peanut butter, maple syrup, oil, and vanilla extract.

Pour the wet mixture into the dry ingredients and stir with a large wooden spoon until just combined, being careful not to overmix (stop when you no longer see dry flour).

Spoon the batter into the doughnut molds, filling up just halfway. Dot about 2 teaspoons (13 g) of jelly around each doughnut and top with the remaining batter, filling just below the top of each mold, ⅛- to ¼-inch (3 to 6 mm) from the top. Bake for 18 to 22 minutes until lightly golden brown around the edges. A toothpick inserted in the center should come out clean. Let cool in the pan for 5 minutes. Slide a thin spatula around the edges of the doughnuts to help loosen them out. Then place on a cooling rack and allow to cool fully before topping.

Finish with a swipe of peanut butter on the cooled doughnuts.

RECIPE NOTE

See page 83 for easy instructions on how to make peanut meal at home.

CHOCOLATE DOUGHNUTS
WITH MEDJOOL DATE CARAMEL SAUCE

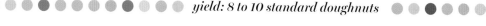

yield: 8 to 10 standard doughnuts

A healthier chocolate doughnut? Can it be? Yes, it can. And it's topped with a thick and sticky caramel made from dates! This doughnut is really going to surprise you.

RECOMMENDED PANS:
Standard, mini, holes, twist

FOR THE DOUGHNUTS:
½ cup (60 g) oat flour
½ cup (56 g) almond meal
¼ cup + 2 tablespoons (76 g) coconut
    sugar or sucanat
¼ cup (35 g) sweet rice flour
3 tablespoons (15 g) unsweetened cocoa
    powder
1½ tablespoons (11 g) ground flax meal
1 teaspoon baking powder
½ teaspoon salt
1 large egg
½ cup (120 ml) milk
¼ cup (60 g) unsweetened applesauce
2 tablespoons (28 ml) unrefined coconut
    oil, melted and slightly cooled
1½ teaspoons vanilla extract

FOR THE SAUCE:
12 medjool dates, pitted and halved
½ cup (120 ml) water
¼ to ½ cup (60 to 120 ml) unsweetened
    almond milk
1 tablespoon (15 ml) melted coconut oil
1 tablespoon (20 g) pure maple syrup
1 teaspoon vanilla bean paste
¼ teaspoon cinnamon
Large flaked sea salt

TO MAKE THE DOUGHNUTS: Preheat your oven to 350°F (180°C, or gas mark 4) and grease your doughnut pan.

Combine the oat flour, almond meal, coconut sugar, sweet rice flour, cocoa powder, flax meal, baking powder, and salt in a large bowl, mixing well. In another bowl, whisk the egg. Then whisk in the milk, applesauce, oil, and vanilla extract.

Pour the wet mixture into the dry ingredients and stir with a large wooden spoon until just combined, being careful not to overmix (stop when you no longer see dry flour).

Spoon the batter into the doughnut molds, filling to just below the top of each mold, ⅛- to ¼-inch (3 to 6 mm) from the top. Bake for 18 to 22 minutes until lightly golden brown around the edges. A toothpick inserted in the center should come out clean. Let cool in the pan for 5 minutes. Slide a thin spatula around the edges of the doughnuts to help loosen them out. Then place on a cooling rack and allow to cool fully before topping.

TO MAKE THE SAUCE: Soak the dates in warm water for 1 hour and then drain. Place in a high-speed blender with ½ cup (120 ml) water and ¼ cup (60 ml) milk, along with the oil, maple syrup, vanilla bean paste, and cinnamon. Blend starting on low and working up to high, scraping the sides down as needed. Blend until creamy, smooth, and spreadable. The sauce will not be drippy or pourable. Add more milk as needed. Spread on the doughnuts, top with a sprinkle of sea salt, and serve.

PISTACHIO HONEY DOUGHNUTS
WITH CRUNCHY ROASTED PISTACHIOS

yield: 6 to 8 standard doughnuts

If there were one nut that fits the "once you pop you can't stop" saying, it would be pistachios. Why are they so addictive? I can't answer that, but I can tell you the same applies to these doughnuts. Pistachio is my mom's favorite ice cream flavor, so I couldn't help but create a pistachio doughnut for my mom and all the other pistachio lovers out there.

RECOMMENDED PANS:
Standard, mini, holes, twist

FOR THE DOUGHNUTS:
½ cup (60 g) oat flour
¼ cup (70 g) sweet rice flour
¼ cup (28 g) pistachio meal
¼ cup (28 g) almond meal
2 tablespoons (14 g) ground flax meal
1 teaspoon baking powder
½ teaspoon salt
1 large egg
⅓ cup (80 ml) milk
¼ cup (80 g) honey
¼ cup (60 g) unsweetened applesauce
1 tablespoon (15 ml) oil
1½ teaspoons vanilla extract

FOR THE TOPPING:
¾ cup (112 g) ground roasted pistachios, unsalted
⅛ teaspoon salt
½ cup (160 g) honey

TO MAKE THE DOUGHNUTS: Preheat your oven to 350°F (180°C, or gas mark 4) and grease your doughnut pan.

Combine the oat flour, sweet rice flour, pistachio meal, almond meal, flax meal, baking powder, and salt in a large bowl, mixing well. In another bowl, whisk the egg. Then whisk in the milk, honey, applesauce, oil, and vanilla extract.

Pour the wet mixture into the dry ingredients and stir with a large wooden spoon until just combined, being careful not to overmix (stop when you no longer see dry flour).

Spoon the batter into the doughnut molds, filling to just below the top of each mold, ⅛- to ¼-inch (3 to 6 mm) from the top. Bake for 18 to 22 minutes until lightly golden brown around the edges. A toothpick inserted in the center should come out clean. Let cool in the pan for 5 minutes. Slide a thin spatula around the edges of the doughnuts to help loosen them out. Then place on a cooling rack and allow to cool fully before topping.

TO MAKE THE TOPPING: In a bowl, mix the pistachios and salt together. Bring the honey to a simmer over medium heat and transfer to a small bowl big enough to dip the doughnut into. Carefully (honey will be very hot!) dip the top of each doughnut in the honey and let any excess drip off. Place on a cooling rack and top each doughnut with the ground pistachios. Let cool and serve.

RECIPE NOTE

Pistachio meal can be made at home by following the same instructions for making almond meal on page 11. Use unsalted, shelled pistachios.

CINNAMON RAISIN OAT DOUGHNUTS
WITH CRUNCHY GRANOLA TOPPING

yield: 10 to 12 standard doughnuts

I've always been a fan of granola, whether it's in a bowl with milk, on top of yogurt, or straight from the bag. The toasted oats, the honey sweetness, the nuts, raisins, and cinnamon make it completely addictive. In this doughnut, I've tried to capture my favorite granola components through and through.

RECOMMENDED PANS:
Standard, mini, twist

FOR THE DOUGHNUTS:
½ cup (60 g) oat flour
½ cup (56 g) almond meal
⅓ cup (27 g) rolled oats
¼ cup (35 g) sweet rice flour
2 tablespoons (14 g) ground flax meal
1½ teaspoons cinnamon
1 teaspoon baking powder
½ teaspoon salt
1 large egg
¼ cup + 2 tablespoons (88 ml) milk
¼ cup (80 g) pure maple syrup
¼ cup (45 g) unsweetened applesauce
1 tablespoon (15 m) oil
2 teaspoons vanilla extract
⅓ cup (50 g) raisins

FOR THE TOPPING:
¾ cup (195 g) creamy roasted almond
    butter, softened
2 tablespoons (40 g) pure maple syrup,
    warmed
Gluten-free granola (optional)

TO MAKE THE DOUGHNUTS: Preheat your oven to 350°F (180°C, or gas mark 4) and grease your doughnut pan.

Combine the oat flour, almond meal, rolled oats, sweet rice flour, ground flax, cinnamon, baking powder, and salt in a bowl, mixing well. In another bowl, whisk the egg. Then whisk in the milk, maple syrup, applesauce, oil, and vanilla extract.

Pour the wet mixture into the dry ingredients and stir with a large wooden spoon until just combined, being careful not to overmix (stop when you no longer see dry flour). Gently fold in the raisins.

Spoon the batter into the doughnut molds, filling to just below the top of each mold, ⅛- to ¼-inch (3 to 6 mm) from the top. Bake for 18 to 22 minutes until lightly golden brown around the edges. A toothpick inserted in the center should come out clean. Let cool in the pan for 5 minutes. Slide a thin spatula around the edges of the doughnuts to help loosen them out. Then place on a cooling rack and allow to cool fully before topping.

TO MAKE THE TOPPING: Mix ingredients together until smooth. Spread over the doughnuts and sprinkle crushed gluten-free granola over top.

CHAPTER 9

more than a doughnut

FUN AND DELICIOUS CREATIONS WITH DOUGHNUTS!

· ·

Did you ever think you would see a five-layer cake made out of doughnuts? What about doughnut bread pudding or doughnut eggs benedict? In this chapter, you will find recipes that stretch the doughnut imagination. You may even find a recipe for your furry friends. Get ready. It's a fun one!

· ·

BUCKEYE DOUGHNUT ICE CREAM
WITH PEANUT BUTTER DOUGHNUT CHUNKS

yield: 1 generous quart

To make this ice cream, I referred to the great Jeni of Jeni's Splendid Ice Creams. Not only is her ice cream the best I've ever tasted, but her fame began right down the street from my alma mater, Ohio State. I had to create this spin of her Buckeye State ice cream. It is absolutely packed with flavor. From the vanilla beans, to the peanut butter swirl, to the slight chocolate crunch and the soft peanut butter doughnuts packed inside, it's a keeper.

2 cups (475 ml) whole milk

I tablespoon + I teaspoon (II g) tapioca starch

3 tablespoons (45 g) cream cheese, softened

⅓ cup (87 g) natural creamy peanut butter

1¼ cups (195 ml) heavy cream

⅔ cup (133 g) pure cane sugar

3 tablespoons (60 g) clover honey

I vanilla bean pod, scraped

¼ to ½ teaspoon salt

½ batch Peanut Butter Cup Doughnuts (page 83), cut into chunks

½ cup (88 g) chopped dark chocolate

Whisk 2 tablespoons (28 ml) of the whole milk with the tapioca starch until smooth.

In a large bowl, mix the cream cheese and peanut butter together with a fork until well combined. The mixture will be thick.

Prepare a large bowl with water and ice. Also place a fine-mesh strainer over a medium bowl.

In a medium saucepan, whisk together the remaining milk, cream, sugar, honey, vanilla beans, and salt. Add the scraped pod and bring the mixture to a rapid boil over medium-high heat. Boil for 4 minutes, stirring occasionally. Reduce the heat if the mixture starts to boil over.

Remove from the heat and slowly pour in the starch mixture while whisking until smooth. Place back over medium-high heat and return to a boil for about I minute, stirring constantly until the mixture just starts to thicken. Remove from the heat and pour through a fine-mesh strainer and discard the vanilla bean.

Slowly whisk the milk mixture into the cream cheese mixture until smooth. Pour the mixture into a gallon-size (3.8 L) sealable plastic bag. Place the entire sealed bag in the ice bath for at least 30 minutes or until fully chilled. Add more ice if needed.

Pour the ice cream mixture into your ice cream maker and turn on. Just before the ice cream is finished mixing (refer to your ice cream maker manual), add in the chocolate and half of the doughnut pieces, letting spin for I minute.

Pour into an airtight container in 4 increments and add ¼ cup of the doughnut pieces after each addition, packing down each time. Place a piece of plastic wrap directly on top of the ice cream and seal the container. Freeze for 4 to 6 hours before serving.

DOUGHNUT STACKED BIRTHDAY CAKE
WITH BUTTERCREAM FROSTING

yield: 1 cake

Can you imagine this cake being set down in front of you on your birthday? There are so many ways you can customize this cake. From using a variety of different doughnut flavor recipes, to topping it with a drip glaze, or maybe a maple infused buttercream frosting, the sky's the limit with this crowd-pleaser.

25 doughnuts of your choosing
  (3 to 4 batches)
2½ to 3½ cups (820 g to 1.1 kg) of your
  favorite buttercream frosting
Sprinkles

Spread the frosting smoothly on each doughnut with a small offset spatula. Place 5 frosted doughnuts on a large plate or cake stand for the first layer, making sure they are touching and form a circle.

Continue to frost doughnuts and place directly on top of the doughnuts below. Stop when you have frosted all 5 layers. Top with sprinkles.

RECIPE NOTE

You can also glaze this cake (with a triple batch of glaze) by lightly dipping the top of each doughnut into glaze and letting the excess drip off. Stack in layers of 5 as described above. After all 5 layers are stacked, drizzle more glaze on the top and down the sides of the cake to finish.

FRENCH TOAST DOUGHNUT BREAD PUDDING
WITH BROWN SUGAR PECAN OAT TOPPING

yield: 6 to 8 servings

I don't even know how this idea came to be, but it's not surprising seeing as I've been a bread pudding fan all my life. After removing it from the oven, I waited zero seconds before diving in with a fork and then proceeded to polish off nearly half the pan. Oops.

FOR THE DOUGHNUTS:

2 batches of French Toast Doughnuts,
   cooled (page 160)
3 large eggs
1½ cups (355 ml) whole milk
¼ cup (80 g) pure maple syrup
1½ teaspoons vanilla extract
1½ teaspoons cinnamon

FOR THE TOPPING:

½ cup (40 g) rolled oats
¼ cup (60 g) packed brown sugar
3 tablespoons (42 g) butter, softened
⅓ cup (37 g) chopped pecans

Preheat your oven to 350°F (180°C, or gas mark 4) and grease a 9 x 9 inch (23 x 23 cm) pan.

Break each doughnut apart into 4 or 5 pieces and place in a large bowl. In another bowl, whisk together the eggs. Then whisk in the milk, maple syrup, vanilla extract, and cinnamon until fully combined. Pour over the doughnuts and gently fold the mixture together a few times with a large spoon or spatula. You want the doughnuts to be lightly coated but left as intact as possible. It will become slightly crumbly.

Mash the oats, brown sugar, and butter together in a bowl. Once combined, mix in the pecans.

Pour the doughnut mixture into the greased pan, making sure to pour out all of the liquid. Spread in an even layer and sprinkle with the brown sugar topping. Cover tightly with foil and bake for 35 minutes. Uncover and bake for 10 minutes until light golden brown and the top starts to crisp. Broil for a few minutes if desired, but watch carefully.

Let sit for 5 to 10 minutes and then serve.

BANANA BREAD DOUGHNUT PANCAKES
WITH BANANA WALNUT MAPLE TOPPING

yield: about 6 to 8 pancakes

Are you finally ready to love gluten-free pancakes? With this recipe you surely will and so will anyone else who tries them. The banana bread flavors are comforting and perfect for breakfast, especially when topped with a nut crunch, a dab of butter, and a drizzle of maple syrup.

FOR THE PANCAKES:
½ cup (60 g) oat flour
¼ cup (35 g) sweet rice flour
¼ cup (28 g) almond meal
1½ tablespoons (20 g) pure cane sugar
1¼ teaspoons cinnamon
1 teaspoon baking powder
½ teaspoon salt
2 large eggs
¼ cup + 2 tablespoons (88 ml) milk
⅓ cup (75 g) well-mashed banana
1 tablespoon (15 ml) oil
1 teaspoon vanilla extract

FOR THE TOPPING:
Sliced banana
Chopped walnuts
Butter
Pure maple syrup

Combine the oat flour, sweet rice flour, almond meal, cane sugar, cinnamon, baking powder, and salt in a large bowl, mixing until well combined.

Place the eggs, milk, banana, oil, and vanilla extract into a blender and blend until smooth.

Pour the wet mixture into the dry ingredients and stir with a large wooden spoon until just combined, being careful not to overmix (stop when you no longer see dry flour). Let rest for 5 minutes. The batter should be thick but pourable.

Heat a large pan or griddle over medium to medium-low heat. Add a bit of butter or coconut oil to coat the pan. Once hot, spoon about ¼ cup (55 g) of the batter into the pan, forming 5- to 6-inch (13 to 15 cm) pancakes. Do not overcrowd the pan. For extra fun, spoon the batter into a circular doughnut-shaped pancake. Cook for 2 to 4 minutes until you see bubbles popping at the surface. Carefully flip with a large spatula and cook for another 2 to 3 minutes.

Serve warm with sliced bananas, walnuts, butter, and maple syrup.

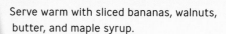

VEGETARIAN EGGS BENEDICT
WITH DAIRY-FREE HOLLANDAISE SAUCE

yield: 6 to 8 standard doughnuts

The English muffin is no longer necessary with this simple doughnut recipe as the new base for this breakfast staple. It's topped with a dairy-free, vegan hollandaise sauce that will have you dunking everything in sight into this sauce. It's perfect for a Sunday brunch!

RECOMMENDED PANS:
Standard

FOR THE DOUGHNUTS:
½ cup (60 g) oat flour
½ cup (70 g) sweet rice flour
3 tablespoons (21 g) almond meal
I teaspoon baking powder
¾ teaspoon salt
½ teaspoon black pepper
2 large eggs
⅓ cup (80 ml) milk
¼ cup (77 g) plain Greek yogurt
3 tablespoons (45 ml) oil

FOR THE VEGAN HOLLANDAISE:
I cup (230 g) cashew cream (page 128)
I tablespoon (15 ml) lemon juice
I tablespoon (6 g) nutritional yeast
¼ teaspoon salt
¼ teaspoon black pepper
¼ teaspoon turmeric
⅛ to ¼ teaspoon cayenne pepper

FOR THE TOPPING:
Spinach
Avocado
Poached eggs
Salt and pepper

TO MAKE THE DOUGHNUTS: Preheat your oven to 350°F (180°C, or gas mark 4) and grease your doughnut pan.

Combine the oat flour, sweet rice flour, almond meal, baking powder, salt, and black pepper in a large bowl, mixing well. In another bowl, whisk the eggs together. Then whisk in the milk, yogurt, and oil.

Pour the wet mixture into the dry ingredients and stir with a large wooden spoon until just combined, being careful not to overmix (stop when you no longer see dry flour).

Spoon the batter into the doughnut molds, filling to just below the top of each mold, ⅛- to ¼-inch (3 to 6 mm) from the top. Bake for 18 to 22 minutes until lightly golden brown around the edges. A toothpick inserted in the center should come out clean. Let cool in the pan for 5 minutes. Slide a thin spatula around the edges of the doughnuts to help loosen them out. Then place on a cooling rack and allow to cool fully.

TO MAKE THE SAUCE: Place all sauce ingredients in your blender and blend until smooth. Taste and add more salt, pepper, or cayenne pepper if needed. Pour into a saucepan and heat over medium-low heat until warm, stirring frequently.

TO ASSEMBLE THE DOUGHNUTS: Lightly toast the doughnuts on each side in a toaster or oven. Carefully remove the doughnuts. Place on a spinach-topped plate. Layer on the avocado slices, the poached egg, and then the hollandaise. Top with a sprinkle of salt and black pepper to finish.

RECIPE NOTE

For a vegan version, use the Vegan Garlic Spinach Doughnuts (page 119) and replace the egg with grilled or baked tofu!

FRENCH TOAST DOUGHNUTS
WITH BUTTER AND MAPLE SYRUP

yield: 6 to 8 standard doughnuts,
or 12 to 16 half slices of French toast

French toast will always be my favorite breakfast meal. Did you ever imagine it would be made with doughnuts? A lightly sweetened doughnut is sliced in half, then dredged in a cinnamon egg mixture and cooked to a browned perfection. Your French toast breakfast just got a facelift.

RECOMMENDED PANS:
Standard

FOR THE DOUGHNUTS:
½ cup (60 g) oat flour
½ cup (70 g) sweet rice flour
3 tablespoons (19 g) almond meal
1 teaspoon baking powder
1 teaspoon cinnamon
½ teaspoon salt
2 large eggs
⅓ cup (80 ml) milk
¼ cup (60 g) unsweetened applesauce
2 tablespoons (40 g) pure maple syrup
2 tablespoons (28 g) butter, melted and
    slightly cooled
1½ teaspoons vanilla extract

FOR THE EGG MIXTURE:
3 large eggs
⅓ cup (80 ml) whole milk
½ teaspoon cinnamon
1 teaspoon vanilla extract

FOR THE FRENCH TOAST:
Unrefined coconut oil, or butter
Maple syrup

TO MAKE THE DOUGHNUTS: Preheat your oven to 350°F (180°C, or gas mark 4) and grease your doughnut pan.

Combine the oat flour, sweet rice flour, almond meal, baking powder, cinnamon, and salt in a large bowl, mixing well. In another bowl, whisk the eggs together. Then whisk in the milk, applesauce, maple syrup, butter, and vanilla extract.

Pour the wet mixture into the dry ingredients and stir with a large wooden spoon until just combined, being careful not to overmix (stop when you no longer see dry flour).

Spoon the batter into the doughnut molds, filling to just below the top of each mold, ⅛- to ¼-inch (3 to 6 mm) from the top. Bake for 18 to 22 minutes until lightly golden brown around the edges. A toothpick inserted in the center should come out clean. Let cool in the pan for 5 minutes. Slide a thin spatula around the edges of the doughnuts to help loosen them out. Then place on a cooling rack and allow to cool fully.

TO MAKE THE FRENCH TOAST: Place a large pan or griddle over medium heat and liberally grease with either oil or butter. In a bowl, whisk the eggs together. Then whisk in the milk, cinnamon, and vanilla extract.

Carefully slice each doughnut in half with a small serrated knife. Dip doughnuts into the egg mixture on both sides, letting the excess drip off, and place immediately on the pan.

Cook for 2 to 5 minutes per side until the surface is golden brown and the egg is fully cooked. Grease the pan as needed and continue with the rest of the doughnuts.

Serve warm with butter or coconut oil and maple syrup.

GRILLED CHEESE DOUGHNUTS
WITH YOUR FAVORITE MELTY CHEESE

yield: 6 to 8 standard doughnuts

A simple savory doughnut is stuffed with your favorite cheese, smeared with butter, and grilled in a pan. The outside forms a nice crispiness, while the inside pulls apart with hot, melted cheese. This is a definite contender to be dunked in a bowl of tomato soup. Just an idea. . .

RECOMMENDED PANS:
Standard

FOR THE DOUGHNUTS:
½ cup (60 g) oat flour
½ cup (70 g) sweet rice flour
3 tablespoons (21 g) almond meal
1 teaspoon baking powder
½ teaspoon salt
¼ teaspoon garlic powder
¼ teaspoon black pepper
2 large eggs
⅓ cup (80 ml) buttermilk
3 tablespoons (45 ml) oil
3 tablespoons (45 g) plain yogurt

FOR THE GRILLED CHEESE:
Your favorite cheese, sliced
Butter

TO MAKE THE DOUGHNUTS: Preheat your oven to 350°F (180°C, or gas mark 4) and grease your doughnut pan.

Combine the oat flour, sweet rice flour, almond meal, baking powder, salt, garlic powder, and black pepper in a large bowl, mixing well. In another bowl, whisk the eggs together. Then whisk in the buttermilk, oil, and yogurt.

Pour the wet mixture into the dry ingredients and stir with a large wooden spoon until just combined, being careful not to overmix (stop when you no longer see dry flour).

Spoon the batter into the doughnut molds, filling to just below the top of each mold, ⅛- to ¼-inch (3 to 6 mm) from the top. Bake for 18 to 22 minutes until lightly golden brown around the edges. A toothpick inserted in the center should come out clean. Let cool in the pan for 5 minutes. Slide a thin spatula around the edges of the doughnuts to help loosen them out. Then place on a cooling rack and allow to cool fully.

TO MAKE THE GRILLED CHEESE: Carefully slice each doughnut half with a small serrated knife. Place a pan or griddle over medium heat. Butter each outer-side of the doughnuts and place sliced cheese in the middle. Once the pan is hot, place the filled dough-nut in the pan and cook for 4 to 6 minutes until golden brown. Carefully flip over with a spatula and grill on the other side for 3 to 5 minutes until golden brown. Slice in half and serve warm.

DOG DOUGHNUTS
WITH SLOBBER-KISSED COATING

yield: 36 to 42 doughnut cookies,
plus doughnut cookie holes

This recipe was tested and approved by Dakota and Kenna and their dog friends, Penny and Rita. Trust me when I tell you they won't last long. Who knew making dog treats could be this simple? Make an extra batch and pass them out to your pet-loving neighbors (just make sure you tell them they're for the dogs).

3 to 3½ cups (360 to 420 g) oat flour
½ cup (56 g) ground flax meal
½ teaspoon salt
I large egg
½ cup (130 g) peanut butter, melted
½ cup (123 g) pumpkin purée
3 tablespoons (60 g) molasses

Preheat your oven to 350°F (180°C, or gas mark 4) and line 2 large baking sheets with parchment paper.

Combine 3 cups (360 g) oat flour, ground flax, and salt in a large bowl, mixing well. In another bowl, whisk the egg and then stir in the peanut butter, pumpkin purée, and molasses until fully combined and smooth.

Pour the wet mixture into the dry ingredients and stir with a large wooden spoon until it becomes too hard to stir. Use your hands to incorporate the ingredients together and knead into a giant ball of dough. If the dough is too sticky, knead in more oat flour 2 tablespoons (15 g) at a time.

Liberally flour the surface you're going to roll the dough out on. Remove the dough from the bowl and continue to knead, if necessary, until the dough is stiff but not sticky or crumbly.

Roll half of the dough out to about ⅛ inch (3 mm) thickness and using a 3-inch (7.5 cm) doughnut cookie cutter, biscuit cutter, or 2 lids (3 inches [7.5 cm] and ¾ inch wide [2 cm] wide) cut the cookies from the dough.

Carefully transfer the cookies with a spatula to the baking sheets one by one. Place the doughnut cookies and cookie holes close together but not touching. Knead the excess dough into a ball and roll out again. Cut out the doughnut cookies, transfer them to the baking sheet, and repeat this process until you have no more dough left.

Bake for 30 to 35 minutes until golden brown and crisp. Let cool fully on the pans. They will crisp more as they sit. Transfer to a jar or sealable bag and store on the counter for 2 to 3 weeks or in the fridge to keep fresh for longer.

MINI DOUGHNUT POPS
WITH CRUNCHY CHOCOLATE COATING

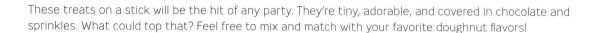

yield: 36 to 48 doughnuts pops

These treats on a stick will be the hit of any party. They're tiny, adorable, and covered in chocolate and sprinkles. What could top that? Feel free to mix and match with your favorite doughnut flavors!

RECOMMENDED PANS:
Mini, holes

FOR THE DOUGHNUTS:
I batch of Vanilla Bean Birthday Doughnuts (page 87), Triple Chocolate Doughnuts (page 104), or Peanut Butter Cup Doughnuts (page 83)
Candy sticks
Sprinkles

FOR THE PEANUT BUTTER CHOCOLATE COATING:
I cup (175 g) dark chocolate chips
3 tablespoons (48 g) creamy peanut butter
I tablespoon (14 g) unrefined coconut oil

FOR THE WHITE CHOCOLATE COATING:
I cup (175 g) white chocolate chips
I tablespoon (14 g) unrefined coconut oil

TO MAKE THE COATINGS: Melt the peanut butter chocolate coating ingredients or the white chocolate coating ingredients using a double boiler method, stirring until smooth. Remove from heat and pour into a small but deep bowl good for dunking.

TO ASSEMBLE THE DOUGHNUT POPS: Gently place a stick through each doughnut and dip the doughnut using a spoon to help coat in chocolate. This will get messy. Place on the parchment-lined pan and let set until the chocolate has hardened. This can be sped up by placing the pops in the fridge for about 15 to 20 minutes.

MINI CAPRESE DOUGHNUT STACKERS
WITH BASIL, MOZZARELLA, AND CHERRY TOMATOES

yield: 26 to 32 mini doughnuts

Caprese skewers will always be one of those go-to party appetizers that everyone is happy to see. They're simple. They're delicious. It only seems right. Now, why not add a mini savory doughnut beneath it all? If you end up eating the entire batch for dinner, I won't tell. I also don't blame you.

RECOMMENDED PANS:
Mini

FOR THE DOUGHNUTS:
½ cup (60 g) oat flour
½ cup (70 g) sweet rice flour
3 tablespoons (21 g) almond meal
1 teaspoon baking powder
¾ teaspoon salt
½ teaspoon dried basil
¼ teaspoon garlic powder
2 large eggs
⅓ cup (80 ml) milk
¼ cup (60 g) unsweetened applesauce
3 tablespoons (45 ml) extra-virgin
  olive oil

FOR THE TOPPING:
Fresh basil leaves
Fresh mozzarella
Cherry tomatoes
Flaked sea salt
Fresh ground black pepper
Drizzle of extra-virgin olive oil (optional)

TO MAKE THE DOUGHNUTS: Preheat your oven to 350°F (180°C, or gas mark 4) and grease your doughnut pan.

Combine the oat flour, sweet rice flour, almond meal, baking powder, salt, basil, and garlic powder in a large bowl, mixing well. In another bowl, whisk the eggs together. Then whisk in the milk, applesauce, and oil.

Pour the wet mixture into the dry ingredients and stir with a large wooden spoon until just combined, being careful not to overmix (stop when you no longer see dry flour).

Spoon the batter into the doughnut molds, filling to just below the top of each mold, ⅛- to ¼-inch (3 to 6 mm) from the top. Bake for 10 to 12 minutes until lightly golden brown around the edges. A toothpick inserted in the center should come out clean. Let cool in the pan for 5 minutes. Slide a thin spatula around the edges of the doughnuts to help loosen them out. Then place on a cooling rack and allow to cool fully before topping.

TO ASSEMBLE THE DOUGHNUTS:
Place the doughnuts on a large platter. Fold a basil leaf in half and place on the doughnut. Next, add a small slice of fresh mozzarella and then a tomato on top. Top with salt and black pepper. Drizzle with olive oil, if desired. Secure with a skewer, if needed.

VEGAN VARIATIONS

GENERAL VEGAN INSTRUCTIONS: *Follow the instructions below for all Vegan recipes, unless otherwise noted.*

TO MAKE THE DOUGHNUTS: Preheat your oven to 350°F (180°C, or gas mark 4) and grease your doughnut pan.

Combine the dry ingredients in a large bowl and stir until combined. In another bowl, whisk all of the wet ingredients together until fully combined.

Pour the wet mixture into the dry ingredients and stir with a large wooden spoon until just combined, being careful not to overmix (stop when you no longer see dry flour). Let sit for 5 minutes. Do not stir after this point. The batter will be very thick and not pourable.

Spoon the batter into the doughnut molds, filling to just below the top of each mold, 1/8- to 1/4-inch (3 to 6 mm) from the top. Lightly smooth out the top of the batter with a small silicone spatula. Do not pack the batter down.

Bake for 18 to 22 minutes until lightly golden brown around the edges. A toothpick inserted in the center should come out clean. Let cool in the pan for 5 minutes. Slide a thin spatula around the edges of the doughnuts to help loosen them out. Then place on a cooling rack and allow to cool fully before topping.

TO MAKE THE FROSTINGS AND GLAZES: Refer to the pages specified for each topping recipe and unless otherwise noted, substitute vegan butter (such as Earth Balance) for dairy butter and unsweetened non-dairy milk (such as soy or almond milk) when milk is called for.

VEGAN BUTTERMILK DOUGHNUTS

 *yield: 6 to 8 standard doughnuts*

FOR THE VEGAN BUTTERMILK:
1/2 cup + 2 tablespoons (148 ml)
   unsweetened almond milk
1 1/2 teaspoons apple cider vinegar

FOR THE DOUGHNUTS:
1/2 cup (60 g) oat flour
1/2 cup (70 g) sweet rice flour
1/3 cup (67 g) pure cane sugar
2 tablespoons (14 g) almond meal
2 tablespoons (14 g) coconut flour
2 tablespoons (14 g) ground flax meal
1 teaspoon baking powder
1/2 teaspoon baking soda
1/2 teaspoon salt
1/4 cup (60 g) unsweetened applesauce

3 tablespoons (45 ml) oil
1 teaspoon vanilla extract

FOR THE TOPPING:
Refer to page 15 for the ingredient list and instructions. Make vegan substitutes as noted in the general vegan instructions.

After preheating the oven, whisk together the milk and vinegar and let sit for 5 minutes until curdled. Proceed with the general vegan instruction above, whisking in with other wet ingredients as directed.

VEGAN CORNBREAD DOUGHNUTS

yield: 8 to 10 standard doughnuts

FOR THE DOUGHNUTS:
⅓ cup (40 g) oat flour
⅓ cup (47 g) fine-grain cornmeal
⅓ cup (39 g) masa harina
3 tablespoons (26 g) sweet rice flour
2 tablespoons (14 g) almond meal
2 tablespoons (14 g) coconut flour
2 tablespoons (14 g) ground flax meal
2 tablespoons (26 g) pure cane sugar
2½ teaspoons (11.5 g) baking powder
½ teaspoon baking soda
½ teaspoon salt
¾ cup (175 ml) unsweetened almond milk
¼ cup (60 g) unsweetened applesauce
3 tablespoons (45 ml) oil
1½ teaspoons vanilla extract

FOR THE TOPPING:
Refer to page 120 for the ingredient list and instructions. Make vegan substitutes as noted in the general vegan instructions.

Follow the general vegan instructions as listed on left page.

VEGAN VANILLA BEAN BIRTHDAY DOUGHNUTS

yield: 8 to 10 standard doughnuts

FOR THE DOUGHNUTS:
½ cup (60 g) oat flour
½ cup (70 g) sweet rice flour
⅓ cup (67 g) pure cane sugar
2 tablespoons (14 g) almond meal
2 tablespoons (14 g) coconut flour
2 tablespoons (14 g) ground flax meal
1 teaspoon baking powder
½ teaspoon baking soda
½ teaspoon salt
½ cup + 2 tablespoons (148 ml) unsweetened almond milk
¼ cup (60 g) unsweetened applesauce
3 tablespoons (45 ml) oil
2 teaspoons vanilla bean paste
⅛ teaspoon almond extract

FOR THE FROSTING:
3 tablespoons (42 g) vegan butter, softened
¾ to 1 cup (90 to 120 g) vegan powdered sugar
2 to 3 tablespoons (28 to 45 ml) unsweetened almond milk
1 teaspoon vanilla bean paste

TO MAKE THE DOUGHNUTS: Follow the general vegan instructions as listed on left page.

TO MAKE THE FROSTING: Beat vegan butter and powdered sugar together until fluffy and smooth. Add the milk and vanilla bean paste and beat until creamy. Spread over the doughnuts and top with sprinkles, if desired.

VEGAN EGGNOG DOUGHNUTS

yield: 8 to 10 standard doughnuts

FOR THE DOUGHNUTS:
½ cup (70 g) oat flour
½ cup (96 g) sweet rice flour
⅓ cup (67 g) pure cane sugar
2 tablespoons (14 g) almond meal
2 tablespoons (14 g) coconut flour
2 tablespoons (14 g) ground flax meal
1 teaspoon baking powder
½ teaspoon baking soda
½ teaspoon salt
½ teaspoon nutmeg
½ cup + 2 tablespoons (148 ml) vegan
   egg nog
¼ cup (60 g) unsweetened applesauce
3 tablespoons (45 ml) oil
2 teaspoons vanilla extract

FOR THE TOPPING:
Refer to page 66 for the ingredient list and instructions. Make vegan substitutes as noted in the general vegan instructions.

Follow the general vegan instructions as listed on page 166.

VEGAN MAPLE DOUGHNUTS

yield: 8 to 10 standard doughnuts

FOR THE DOUGHNUTS:
½ cup (70 g) oat flour
½ cup (70 g) sweet rice flour
3 tablespoons (39 g) pure cane sugar
2 tablespoons (14 g) almond meal
2 tablespoons (14 g) coconut flour
2 tablespoons (14 g) ground flax meal
1 teaspoon baking powder
½ teaspoon baking soda
½ teaspoon salt
¼ teaspoon cinnamon
½ cup (120 ml) unsweetened almond milk
¼ cup (60 g) unsweetened applesauce
3 tablespoons (45 ml) oil
2½ tablespoons (50 g) pure maple syrup
2 teaspoons vanilla extract

FOR THE TOPPING:
Refer to page 21 for the ingredient list and instructions. Make vegan substitutes as noted in the general vegan instructions.

Follow the general vegan instructions as listed on page 166.

VEGAN TRIPLE CHOCOLATE DOUGHNUTS

yield: 8 to 10 standard doughnuts

FOR THE DOUGHNUTS:
½ cup (60 g) oat flour
½ cup (70 g) sweet rice flour
½ cup (100 g) pure cane sugar
¼ cup (20 g) unsweetened cocoa powder
2 tablespoons (14 g) almond meal
2 tablespoons (14 g) coconut flour
2 tablespoons (14 g) ground flax meal
1 teaspoon baking powder
½ teaspoon baking soda
½ teaspoon salt
¾ cup (175 ml) unsweetened almond milk
¼ cup (60 g) unsweetened applesauce
3 tablespoons (45 ml) oil
½ cup (88 g) vegan dark chocolate chips

FOR THE TOPPING:
Refer to page 104 for the ingredient list and instructions. Make vegan substitutes as noted in the general vegan instructions.

Follow the the general vegan instructions as listed on page 166. Gently fold the chocolate chips in right before you let the batter rest for 5 minutes.

VEGAN PUMPKIN SPICE DOUGHNUTS

yield: 8 to 10 standard doughnuts

FOR THE DOUGHNUTS:
½ cup (70 g) oat flour
½ cup (70 g) sweet rice flour
¼ cup + 2 tablespoons (76 g) pure cane sugar
2 tablespoons (14 g) almond meal
2 tablespoons (14 g) coconut flour
2 tablespoons (14 g) ground flax meal
1½ teaspoons cinnamon
1 teaspoon baking powder
½ teaspoon baking soda
½ teaspoon salt
½ teaspoon ginger
½ teaspoon nutmeg
¼ teaspoon allspice
⅛ teaspoon ground cloves

½ cup + 2 tablespoons (148 ml) unsweetened almond milk
⅓ cup (82 g) pumpkin purée
3 tablespoons (45 ml) oil
2 teaspoons vanilla extract

FOR THE TOPPING:
Refer to page 50 for the ingredient list and instructions. Make vegan substitutes as noted in the general vegan instructions.

Follow the general vegan instructions as listed on page 166.

RESOURCES

Below you'll find a helpful guide directing you to many of the ingredients and tools used through the book. All products listed below are free of gluten but may not be certified gluten-free. Please be sure to source certified gluten-free products if necessary. Many of the items are easily found (and often cheapest) on www.amazon.com.

FLOURS AND MEALS

ALMOND FLOUR (BLANCHED)
Honeyville (www.honeyvillegrain.com)

ALMOND MEAL
Natural Grocers by Vitamin Cottage
   (www.naturalgrocers.com)
Trader Joe's (www.traderjoes.com)

COCONUT FLOUR
Bob's Red Mill (www.bobsredmill.com)
Natural Grocers by Vitamin Cottage
   (www.naturalgrocers.com)
Coconut Secret (www.coconutsecret.com)

CORNMEAL
Bob's Red Mill Gluten-Free (www.bobsredmill.com)

GROUND FLAX MEAL
Bob's Red Mill (www.bobsredmill.com)

MASA HARINA
Bob's Red Mill Gluten-Free (www.bobsredmill.com)

OAT FLOUR
Bob's Red Mill Gluten-Free (www.bobsredmill.com)
Cream Hill Estates (www.creamhillestates.com)

SWEET RICE FLOUR
Ener-G (www.ener-g.com)
Koda Farms (www.kodafarms.com)

DOUGHNUT STAPLES

CHOCOLATE CHIPS
Enjoy Life (www.enjoylifefoods.com)
Sunspire (www.sunspire.com)

COCOA POWDER
Equal Exchange (www.equalexchange.coop)

GLUTEN-FREE CHOCOLATE SANDWICH COOKIES
Mi-Del (www.midelcookies.com)

GLUTEN-FREE GRAHAM CRACKERS
Kinnikinnick (www.kinnikinnick.com)

GLUTEN-FREE PEANUT BUTTER PUFFS
Nature's Path Organic EnviroKidz
   (us.naturespath.com)

GREEN MATCHA POWDER BAKING GRADE
Vital Life (www.vitalifematcha.com)

JAM/JELLY
Crofter's Organic (www.croftersorganic.com)

MOLASSES
Wholesome Sweeteners
   (www.wholesomesweeteners.com)

PEANUT BUTTER
Maranatha (www.maranathafoods.com)
Woodstock Farms (www.woodstock-foods.com)

SPRINKLES
India Tree (www.indiatree.com)
Let's Do Organic Sprinklez (www.wholefoods.com)

VANILLA BEANS, EXTRACT, PASTE
Beanilla (www.beanilla.com)
Frontier Co-op (www.frontiercoop.com)
Nielson-Massey (www.nielsenmassey.com)

YOGURT
Stonyfield (www.stonyfield.com)
Wallaby Organic (www.wallabyyogurt.com)

SWEETENERS

CLOVER HONEY
GloryBee (www.glorybee.com)

COCONUT SUGAR
Madhava Natural Sweeteners
   (www.madhavasweeteners.com)

POWDERED SUGAR
Wholesome Sweeteners
   (www.wholesomesweeteners.com)
Woodstock Farms (www.woodstock-foods.com)

PURE CANE SUGAR
Whole Foods 365 (www.wholefoods.com)
Woodstock Farms (www.woodstock-foods.com)

PURE MAPLE SYRUP GRADE B
NOW Foods (www.nowfoods.com)
Whole Foods 365 (www.wholefoods.com)

VEGAN CANE SUGAR
Florida Crystals (www.floridacrystals.com)
Whole Foods 365 (www.wholefoods.com)
Wholesome Sweeteners
    (www.wholesomesweeteners.com)

DAIRY AND NONDAIRY MILK

COCONUT MILK
Thai Kitchen Organic (www.thaikitchen.com)
Trader Joe's (www.traderjoes.com)

CREAM CHEESE
Organic Valley (www.organicvalley.coop)
Nancy's Organic (www.nancysyogurt.com)

HALF-AND-HALF
Kalona SuperNatural (www.kalonasupernatural.com)
Organic Valley (www.organicvalley.coop)

ORGANIC 2% MILK
Kalona SuperNatural (www.kalonasupernatural.com)
Organic Valley (www.organicvalley.coop)
Whole Foods 365 (www.wholefoods.com)

UNSWEETENED ALMOND MILK
Pacific (www.pacificfoods.com)

UNSWEETENED NON-GMO SOY MILK
Earth Balance (www.earthbalancenatural.com)
Eden Organic (www.edenfoods.com)

OIL AND BUTTER

COCONUT BUTTER
Artisana (www.artisanafoods.com)

COCONUT OIL
Artisana (www.artisanafoods.com)
Dr. Bronner's Magic "All-One!"
    (www.drbronner.com)
Jarrow Formulas (www.jarrow.com)

SUNFLOWER OIL OR SAFFLOWER OIL
Napa Valley Naturals (www.napavalleynaturals.com)
Spectrum (www.spectrumorganics.com)

BUTTER
Kalona SuperNatural (www.kalonasupernatural.com)
Organic Valley (www.organicvalley.coop)
Whole Foods 365 (www.wholefoods.com)

VEGAN BUTTER
Earth Balance (www.earthbalancenatural.com)

TOOLS

BLENDER
Vitamix (www.vitamix.com)

DOUGHNUT PANS
Hole: Nordic Ware (www.nordicware.com)
Mini: Wilton (www.wilton.com)
Standard: Wilton (www.wilton.com)
Twist: Wilton (www.wilton.com)

DRY MEASURING CUPS AND SPOONS
Chicago Metallic
    (www.chicagometallicbakeware.com)
Progressive (www.progressiveintl.com)
OXO (www.oxo.com)

FOOD PROCESSOR
Cuisinart (www.cuisinart.com)

LIQUID MEASURING CUPS
OXO (www.oxo.com)
Pyrex (www.pyrexware.com)

SMALL SILICONE SPATULA
Crate and Barrel (www.crateandbarrel.com)
OXO (www.oxo.com)

ZESTER/GRATER
Microplane (www.microplane.com)
OXO (www.oxo.com)

ACKNOWLEDGMENTS

This book could not have been possible without the love, support, and guidance of so many. I can't begin to say how lucky I am to have such amazing people in my life.

Thank you to Amanda Waddell of Fair Winds Press for stumbling on my blog some time ago and creating the vision for this book with me as the author and photographer. Your encouragement and enthusiasm was greatly appreciated. The entire team at Fair Winds Press was a joy to work with. Thank you for helping make my vision for the design come to life!

An immeasurable thank-you to my husband. Your support and love are felt daily. Thank you for keeping a smile on my face and for being my No. 1 doughnut eater. I could not have done this without you. I love you!

To my mom and dad, who have been cheering me on since day one. Thank you for your constant love, generosity, phone calls, emails, surprise packages, and for everything else you do. One word. Lucky.

To the doughnut taste-testers who showed up time and time again and helped eat and evaluate the 101 doughnut creations. Ali, Ann, Aunt Cindy, Chris K., Chris M., Dave, Elizabeth, Eric, Fiona, Jenna, Jon, Kelsey, Krista, Kyle H., Laura, Lauren, Megan, Michelle, Natalie, Pat, and Peter.

To the fabulous readers of my blog, Edible Perspective. Your constant encouragement is more appreciated than you will ever know. You have continued to help me grow throughout the years and get me to where I am today. THANK YOU.

To The Doughnut Group on Facebook. Thank you for listening to my rambling updates, checking out my photos, and just for your general awesomeness. It was helpful knowing I had a group of family and friends who were following the process as I chugged along.

To Alan, Sherie, AJ, and Jenna. Thank you one million times and back again. For everything. Love you always.

Thanks to the fabulous Laura for using her expert photo-taking skills to capture me in my kitchen for this book. Your generosity is always appreciated. I cherish our friendship daily.

Thank you to my sister-in-law Natalie for her millions of doughnut combination ideas and constant positivity. I love you to pieces!

To my lovely friend Ann Hopman, who demanded I write a cookbook since the second day we met. You have given me an endless amount of support and helped push me to realize that anything is possible. Thank you.

ABOUT THE AUTHOR

Ashley McLaughlin is the writer, recipe creator, and photographer behind the blog Edible Perspective. She focuses on gluten-free, vegetarian, and vegan recipes that are appealing to all diets and ages. Ashley is a self-taught photographer who works to capture her recipes in clean and simple ways. A Michigan native, Ashley actually spent most of her years growing up in Ohio and is a proud Ohio State Buckeye. While Ashley holds two degrees in architecture, she is wholeheartedly embracing her new career path in food and photography. Her work has appeared everywhere from *Huffington Post Taste*, to the *New York Times* bestseller *Peas and Thank You*, to *O Magazine*. Ashley currently lives in Colorado with her husband and two pups. In her spare time, you will find her walking the dogs, snowboarding down a mountain, snowshoeing up a mountain, cycling on country roads, biking around town, lifting weights in her home office, photographing everything in sight, eating everything in sight, and hanging out with her friends and family.

INDEX

INDEX

INDEX